T CTICAL
CHRISTIANITY

BECOMING A WARRIOR FOR CHRIST

JERRY L. PETERS, JR.

Publishing assistance provided by:

Life Publishers International
1625 North Robberson Avenue
Springfield, MO 65803 U.S.A.
www.LifePublishers.org

Printed in the U.S.A.

TABLE OF CONTENTS

DEDICATION

Many people have helped me through life and others have made life much more difficult, the latter I will not mention. However, I do want to mention a few of those who have assisted me along the way. That is the benefit of writing a book…you can brag on those who have been there through it all.

It goes without mention, but I will mention it anyway that God is the source of my strength, provision and every other positive word in the English language or any other translation. God IS everything and has without a doubt been the source of everything good in this book. If you do not know Him you should! Thank you, Jesus, for carrying me so many times.

Of course I will thank mom and dad for being there for me. Their encouragement and support have helped me along the way. Dad, who has been the eternal optimist has always found a way to see the brighter side of life. Mom, well she is tenacious; and developing that tenacity in my own life has helped me continue on even in the difficult times.

I want to thank a few friends that have always been there for me and lifted me up when I was down. This is not the entire list, but I will save some others for my future books. So Steve Conway, Rev. Warren Kurtz, Rev. Jim Uhey and Dennie Daughtery…thanks for putting up with me and keeping me on the narrow path. You are all awesome men of God and true warriors of the faith. You are making Daddy proud!

It is also crucial that I place my children on this list. Especially, in this first book. Joshua and Chelsea have both been a joy to my life. Many times they are the ones who gave me a reason to continue on. They too, have had to put up with the ups and downs of my career, my attitude and my injuries. I am so proud to be their father and blessed to see that they have turned out far better than I. I love you both so much.

Last but certainly not least is my wife Cherie. She has been the one who has loved me unconditionally through everything. She has given me our beautiful children, nurtured me when I was hurt, encouraged me when I was down and brought me endless joy in a sometimes unbearable journey. It is also Cherie who has sat alone during all of my missions and deployments. However, she did not sit idle. She took care of our house, cared for our children, sought out her advanced education and supported me in every path that I followed. She also prayed endlessly and has become one of the godliest women I know. She is truly a Proverbs 31 woman and fulfills every part of the scripture. I could never thank her enough for what she has meant to me and can never thank God enough for giving me a wife that is more than I could ask or imagine. I love you Cher, deeper than words could ever express.

INTRODUCTION

The goal of this book is to assist Christians to become the warriors that God meant for them to be and to teach the biblical principles that will prepare them for battle against the powers and principalities of darkness. The powers, that from the beginning of time have sought to interrupt our personal relationships, destroy our world, and ultimately undermine our devotion to God.

Part of the process in completing this task, for the reader, is to explain some details about the vacuum that has been created through generations of weak warriors. This is a dilemma that has been expressed by different writers in different ways for thousands of years.

The Apostle Paul deals with this matter in Romans chapter 14. He explains that because we are each different in our personalities and convictions, we have different ways of applying the things of God. Although Paul does not condemn the weakness of Christians, he does encourage us to at some point move beyond that weakness and into the strength of God. This is accomplished by studying the Word of God and by the effort of Christians to help each other grow in the things of God. Therefore, it is not the purpose of this book to condemn other Christians; instead it is merely a process used to point out different areas of concern. Thereby, helping us to evaluate our lives and grow into effective, strong, and mighty warriors; to be used of God to accomplish His mission on Earth.

In the United States we use the term "politically correct." It is a term that defines our current society, pushing us towards an overly sensitive conscience. A conscience that will likely bring criticism from other believers, as they view some of the statements in this book as an attack. Although it is not my purpose to attack anyone, it is inevitable that others will see this effort as purely that—an attack. However, if we go back to the words and teaching of the Apostles, and even the words of Jesus, we will see that political correctness was not always their goal in speaking about the things of God. Their divine purpose was to speak the truth of God and allow that truth to speak for itself. Therefore, what may appear to some to be condemnation or blame may merely be truth that is beyond the understanding or acceptance of the reader. Truth can be used by the Holy Spirit to bring conviction and understanding to the reader, but only to those who are willing to listen to the Holy Spirit and the truth of God. Therefore, it is left up to you, the reader, to evaluate your own life and determine if any of these words can help you in your personal pilgrimage of faith. Therefore, all who read this compilation of thoughts should do so with an attitude of understanding, looking at the intended purpose of opening the heart of the warrior to the realities of the harsh and unforgiving world in which we live as well as the spiritual battles that we face.

As the author of this book, I will also remind each person that I am not a theologian in any sense of the word, and this is not a complete teaching of any one thing. I am nothing more than just another guy who wants to use my life experience to help others in their walk with Christ. Therefore, this book is not meant to answer every theological question about spiritual warfare, nor is it a complete and perfect guide to any of the issues mentioned. The only perfect and infallible word that is available to us is the Bible. God's Word (the Holy Bible) is perfect in every way and has the answer to every issue and battle we encounter. Therefore, as a fellow Christian warrior I would encourage everyone to not just read God's Word, but to study it so that we may show ourselves worthy of all that God has for us, allowing us to learn the spiritual tactics that we need to become better Christians and, along the way, endeavor to limit the casualties of spiritual warfare.

Are you ready? Are you prepared to overcome the trials that you'll face as you begin confronting the spiritual forces discussed in this book? Are you prepared to stand against the enemy as you grow in spiritual knowledge? Are you willing to be fully committed to become the warrior that God designed you to be? Is the purpose of God's kingdom more important to you than any other task in your life? Then I pray that this book helps you to become all that God wants you to be. If so, it will be for His glory and not for mine.

Ephesians 1:11–12

*In him we have obtained an inheritance, having been predestined
according to the purpose of him who works all things according to the
counsel of his will, so that we who were the first to hope in Christ might
be to the praise of his glory.*

Remember: God can work wonders through a broken and available
vessel.

As you proceed through this study, look at everything with these
thoughts in your mind:

1. Jesus is coming back soon.

2. The facts of Scripture are true.

3. Difficult times are ahead for the people of this world.
   Guaranteed.

4. Each person who claims to be a Christian must be doing God's
   work.

5. In the end days, many will fall away.

Therefore, we must be prepared. We must also pursue this study as
if our lives (temporally and eternally) depend on how we live out our
Christian faith. In addition, the lives of our friends, family, and others
we meet along the journey may also be impacted based on how we
pursue God and our walk with Him.

Take time to really search your heart. Allow God to dig deep into
who you are and determine where you stand today. While doing so, be
brutally honest with yourself. If you hold back now, the changes you
may need will not be realized and you will continue in the facade of
life that may be hindering your spiritual growth. Besides, God sees the

motive of your heart. Therefore, if you are hiding anything, you are only deceiving yourself because He already knows.

What steps must I take to serve God fully, no matter what it costs me? (Luke 10:3)

_____

_____

_____

_____

_____

_____

As I prepare to overcome the trials that I may face because I am pursuing God in a new way, what type of trials may I encounter? (Ephesians 6:12)

_____

_____

_____

_____

_____

As I stand against the enemy and grow in spiritual knowledge, where do I find the strength and power to fight this spiritual battle? (Ephesians 6:10–18)

_____

_____

_____

_____

What steps will I take to become fully committed to God as the warrior He designed me to become? (Proverbs 16:3, Proverbs 3:5–8)

_____

_____

_____

_____

_____

_____

What things am I willing to give up so that I may seek God first and understand His purpose in my life? (Exodus 9:16, Proverbs 19:21)

_____

_____

_____

_____

_____

_____

SPIRITUAL WARFARE PRAYER

Tammy Melton, is a longtime friend of our family and an awesome woman of God. She and her husband Bill run a ministry organization called Legacy Ministries (www.legacyministries. info). A few years ago, Tammy wrote a book called *Loving God with All Five Senses*. In that book, she included the following *Spiritual Warfare Prayer*. Tammy has given me the great privilege of opening this book with that prayer given to her by God. Thank you, Tammy and Bill. May God continue to bless all that you do for His kingdom.

Thank you, Lord, for placing the Helmet of Salvation on my head. It will protect me against any thought-bomb the enemy tries to place in my mind. I will not take them on as my thoughts in the Name of Jesus! I place my thoughts in Your hands. Please forgive me for the thoughts I hold on to that are not of You. I ask You to change my mindset to be more like the mind of Christ. Thank you for transforming me by the renewing of the mind.

Thank you, Lord, for placing the Breastplate of Righteousness on me. It will protect my heart. Lord, I place all my emotions in Your hands. Help me to remember that You are with me regardless if I "feel" it or not. Please forgive me when I fear. Thank you that though my righteousness is as filthy rags, yet You have clothed me with Your righteousness because of what You did at Calvary!

Thank you, Lord, for placing the Belt of Truth on my waist. Please reveal any hindrance or lie I have been holding onto that would keep me from trusting You and replace it with Your truth, oh Lord! Help me to let go of my perspective of the Truth and seek Your perspective knowing that Your truth will set me free! Help me also to have a deaf ear to the lies of Satan and give me ears to hear what the Spirit says.

13

Thank you, Lord, that my feet are shod with the Preparation of the Gospel of Peace. I am being prepared for the calling of God on my life to take the Gospel of Peace to others. Help me to remember that no matter what I go through, You will use the circumstances in my life, both good and bad, to prepare me for the destiny You have chosen for me...thus I can have peace in the midst of the storm. Thank you that every step I take will be in Peace and I can take that Peace to people wherever I go!

Thank you, Lord, for putting within my hand the Shield of Faith whereby I can quench every fiery dart of the wicked one. Help me to remember that faith is the substance of things hoped for, the evidence of things not seen and that without faith it is impossible to please You. Forgive me when I have gone forward in my own strength and abilities instead of totally relying on You. Help me to dwell in the Secret place of the Most High where I will be protected from any onslaught of the enemy.

NO MATTER WHAT I GO THROUGH, YOU WILL USE THE CIRCUMSTANCES IN MY LIFE, BOTH GOOD AND BAD, TO PREPARE ME FOR THE DESTINY YOU HAVE CHOSEN FOR ME.

Thank You, Lord, for giving me the Sword of the Spirit which is the Word of God...the only offensive weapon. All the other armor You give me is for protection, and I thank You for just how protected I really am! This weapon is the only thing I need to combat the enemy. It is really an arsenal of many weapons that are not carnal, but are mighty through God to the pulling down of strongholds. Forgive me when I fail to read and study Your Word when You have prompted me to do so. I choose to read Your Word, meditate on Your Word, memorize Your Word and use Your Word against the enemy in due time. Help me to not fret over what I will say, but to trust Your Spirit to give me just the right Word in the very hour I need it. I do not want to debate Your Word thereby casting pearls before swine, but I will speak Your Word to those who are hungry for it as well as proclaim to the enemy "It is Written!" Remind me also, that my enemy is not flesh and blood...it is not any person, including myself...but it is Satan and all the principalities with him. Therefore, I pray that You would remind me to not let corrupt communication proceed out of my mouth but that which is good to the use of edifying, that it may minister grace unto the hearers.

And having done all, I will stand! Thank You that the battle is not mine, but it is Yours! Thank You for the victory in Christ Jesus who came to destroy the works of the enemy! In reality, the enemy has already been crushed under Your feet by your death and resurrection. He is therefore under my feet as I trust in You and let You dwell in me! I am more than a conqueror through You who love me with a perfect love that casts out all fear! And for that I will ever be grateful!

Spiritual Warfare Prayer
Melton, T.B. Loving God with All Five Senses
(Xulon Press, Incorporated 2007), (4-1-16)

We must understand how the Armor of God protects us. This prayer by Tammy Melton is a great place to begin. It is based on the Scripture in Ephesians 6:10–20. The final few verses declare the boldness and fearlessness that we must carry by the power of God to declare His Word in every aspect of our life.

Read the following verses. Break them down one by one and think about how each one can be used in your daily walk.

Ephesians 6:10–20

Finally, be strong in the Lord and in the strength of his might. Put on the whole armor of God, that you may be able to stand against the schemes of the devil. For we do not wrestle against flesh and blood, but against the rulers, against the authorities, against the cosmic powers over this present darkness, against the spiritual forces of evil in the heavenly places. Therefore take up the whole armor of God, that you may be able to withstand in the evil day, and having done all, to stand firm. Stand therefore, having fastened on the belt of truth, and having put on the breastplate of righteousness, and, as shoes for your feet, having put on the readiness given by the gospel of peace. In all circumstances take up the shield of faith, with which you can extinguish all the flaming darts of the evil one; and take the helmet of salvation, and the sword of the Spirit, which is the word of God, praying at all times in the Spirit, with all prayer and supplication. To that end keep alert with all perseverance, making supplication for all the saints, and also for me, that words may be given to me in opening my mouth boldly to proclaim the mystery of the gospel, for which I am an ambassador in chains, that I may declare it boldly, as I ought to speak.

Now let's look at the specific pieces of armor and see how they relate to our spiritual battle. After each one, write down some of the ways you can use each piece.

The Helmet of Salvation is placed on my head. It protects my mind, guides my thoughts, brings redemption, and renews my mind. In what specific ways does the helmet benefit me?

_____

_____

_____

_____

_____

_____

The Breastplate of Righteousness goes around my chest. How does righteousness change my life? How can my emotions control me without God's help? In what ways can my feelings deceive me?

_____

_____

_____

_____

_____

Place the Belt of Truth on my waist. How do lies impact my trust in God? Whose perspective of truth is real truth? How does the truth set me free?

_____

_____

_____

_____

Place the Preparation of the Gospel of Peace on my feet. What dangers and traps lurk on my current path? How can God use my wounds to fulfill His divine plan for my life? How can I walk in peace when I am hurting?

_____

_____

_____

_____

_____

I take up the Shield of Faith in my hand. What is the purpose of faith? How does faith spur me on in battle? What happens when my faith wavers?

_____

_____

_____

_____

_____

In my other hand I grab the Sword of the Spirit, which is the Word of God. How do I use the Sword to attack the enemy? What steps do I take to learn the effectiveness of the Sword in my life? What are the Sword's capabilities? Who is the Master Swordsman that can teach me?

_____

_____

_____

_____

_____

Lord Your Word declares that after I have put on the armor of God, I now stand! I know that this battle is not mine to win but Yours, and my victory is secured by the death and resurrection of Jesus Christ. Lord, help me to be more than a conqueror through You and realize that I am a warrior of the King of Kings. Lord, I will walk in Your might and by Your perfect power. Amen!

THE FACES OF WAR

1

As I begin this book, I know that many of us are familiar with the concept of war. Whether from news clips, movies, or our own personal experience, we have developed an understanding of human conflict. In the midst of that conflict, there are many different viewpoints, opinions, and realities that are formed. While one person may see the conflict as necessary, another may see it as insane. Many outside the combat zone will develop opinions based on their perception of what is going on or from input they have received from sources with hidden agendas. However, without having boots on the ground no one can determine the true reality or scope of the situation. In fact, most people outside the area of operations do not understand what is really going on anyway. Even those who develop their perspective based on information that they have gathered from intelligence, media, or someone they know on the front lines can never understand what those on the ground are enduring. The stark reality is that no matter how information is gathered or how extensive it may be, the only people who really understand the significance of the conflict are those that are plunged into the middle of the fight.

Who are the real victims that get "caught in the middle?" It may be a soldier on one side or the other. It could be a parent, brother, sister, spouse, child, or friend of a combatant. Or it could even be those innocent civilians who have been stuck in the midst of their nation's struggle. These are the ones who take shelter every day from bullets, bombs, and enemies who fight all around their once peaceful home. They are not part of the fight, and they don't want their land destroyed. They may not even know why all of this is happening, but one reality remains: they too are in a fight for their life.

As we look at warfare, we also have to face one very real fact: war means death. Throughout history the conflicts between kingdoms, tribes, or nations have always resulted in the death of innocent victims and warriors alike. Proving again and again that when powers collide, people die. However, after-action reports show that some casualties could have been avoided by the use of proper tactics, better implementation of weapons, clear communication, better trained soldiers, and more defined use of battle assets.

JUST AS THERE ARE CASUALTIES IN PHYSICAL WARFARE, THERE ARE CASUALTIES IN SPIRITUAL WARFARE.

At this point you may be asking, "Why is this guy talking about war and death in a book that is supposed to be about spiritual warfare?" That answer is very simple. War on this earth, that takes place between nations, has many common attributes to the concept and reality of spiritual warfare. A fact this is not lost in the direction that God gave to those He inspired in the writing of Scripture.

Just look at the examples in God's Word. As Israel faces the Philistine army, they send forth a champion named Goliath. This giant warrior of a man defies the people of God and calls for someone to meet him on the battlefield. He even concedes that whoever loses will subject their army to defeat and slavery, but no man comes forth from Israel until a scrawny young shepherd boy named David responds to the challenge. David approaches the giant warrior, who is holding weapons that are almost as big as David himself, yet without fear, David moves forward with a simple slingshot, several stones, and the awesome power of God. Then David defeats the giant and brings victory to Israel.

What an example of our limitations and total dependence upon God as Christians today. Here, we stand with the very power of God to overcome any issue in life. The power to face giants and win against their advanced weapons with a simple rock and a slingshot. Yet we cower to a nation making laws against the Bible, leadership denying prayer in schools, and legislation that removes Scripture verses from our courts and government buildings. Have we forgotten that this land was established by Christians for the freedom of our faith? Where is our little David today? Who is going to step up and take on the giant and lead the Army of God into battle? Is it you? Has your life prepared you for such a time as this? Or do you just feel like you are caught in the middle of the fight?

Like physical warfare, spiritual warfare has those people who are "caught in the middle." Some of those trapped by war are the spiritual warriors fighting the battles through outreach, prayer, and ministry efforts. Others are the innocent ones who are ignorant to what is going on around them. Then there are the ones who just do not want to believe that we are even in a battle, an ignorance that may eventually extract from them and their family an eternal price. Finally, there are those who are the parent, brother, sister, spouse, child, or friend of the warrior who gaze on helplessly as those fighting the spiritual battles are being destroyed.

Spiritual warfare, like physical warfare, also has a variety of viewpoints, opinions, and realities. There are those who speak from truth and experience trying to help others understand, so that they may fight against the evil that seeks to destroy them. Then there are others who spread untruth that is justified only by their ignorance, pride, and arrogance as they follow their own agenda, an agenda that many times has been drafted by the devil himself.

These are just some of the reasons why the attributes of physical battle mimic the spiritual warfare that surrounds all of mankind. The Bible tells us that we face an enemy that seeks to steal, kill and destroy (John 10:10). An enemy that is relentless as he searches out our weakness and plans our destruction (1 Peter 5:8). This is not only a definition of spiritual warfare, but also encompasses the concepts of physical battle. Furthermore, just as there are casualties in physical warfare there are casualties in spiritual warfare, casualties that in some cases can be avoided.

So how do we move away from a victim mentality and being caught in the middle of the battle? In what way can we become a warrior for God and do our part to fight the enemies of God and man?

BATTLE PLAN

WE MUST

1. Make a determined decision to follow God's plan for our lives.

2. Believe Scriptures that tell us God's plan has been designed specifically for each person since the beginning of time.

3. Trust in God's promise that His divine plan will prosper us and not harm us.

4. Understand His plan will take us to the very limits of our existence and replace our struggle with perfect peace and contentment as we follow Him.

5. Set aside our own ways and place our will in the very hands of the almighty God.

In what ways have I been victimized by the things of this world?

How can God help me to overcome those issues in my life? (Galatians 5:16)

What can I do in my daily walk that will have a positive kingdom effect on my society and my circle of influence? (1 Timothy 4:12)

What steps can I take to become more determined to complete God's plan for my life?

_____

_____

_____

_____

_____

_____

What is God's plan for my life, and what steps can I take to follow through with that plan? (Jeremiah 1:5)

_____

_____

_____

_____

_____

_____

PLANNING FOR WAR

2

In physical warfare, there are years of planning that take place before the first round is ever fired. Nations spy on nations, trying to determine their strengths and weaknesses. Intelligence is gathered from those who live in and around the area, as one country prepares to invade another.

Today, we also have the advantage of satellite surveillance, unmanned drones, and pictures that show every detail of the pending area of operations. Just prior to the attack, advance teams are sent in to scout out approaches, locate key targets, and even sabotage hindrances to the coming event.

Finally, the day of attack comes. Those who have planned initiate their plan with the commanders and boots on the ground. The soldiers and leaders who have trained for years follow the orders and initiate their efforts based on a combined effort of man. Yes, long before the war begins, there are many plans that take place.

God's plan is the same way. The spiritual wars that we fight today have been long awaited affairs in the spiritual realm. They have been prophesied and are now coming to fruition.

In each case, God has previously developed a plan to overcome every obstacle the enemy has to initiate. It is a plan that has been displayed throughout history and has never changed, and it has all revolved around His desire to have a loving relationship with His creation. To accomplish that goal and to fulfill His divine purpose, He has used difficult situations to meet the personal and spiritual needs of others. Although His success and victory is guaranteed, it is only possible for us to succeed if we become faithful, willing, and obedient servants to the Lord. We can do this by developing a sense of honor and duty to God that goes beyond our personal wants and desires. As we search out His will for our lives and seek Him, we will begin to see the many wonderful things that He has for each and every person.

To understand God's plan, we must realize that we are all born into a sinful nature. The Apostle Paul tells us in Galatians 5:17 that our fleshly desires are in conflict with the goals of God's Spirit.

Galatians 5:17

For the desires of the flesh are against the Spirit, and the desires of the Spirit are against the flesh, for these are opposed to each other, to keep you from doing the things you want to do.

He explains in 2 Corinthians 4 that the mind of the unbeliever is blinded and that we cannot see the gospel of light that displays the glory of Christ.

2 Corinthians 4:4

In their case the god of this world has blinded the minds of the unbelievers, to keep them from seeing the light of the gospel of the glory of Christ, who is the image of God.

However, if we believe in God's promise and apply His truth to our lives, we are able to move beyond this spiritual blindness. This is a fact declared in the Old Testament through the Prophet Isaiah:

Isaiah 42:16

And I will lead the blind in a way that they do not know, in paths that they have not known I will guide them. I will turn the darkness before them into light, the rough places into level ground. These are the things I do, and I do not forsake them.

As previously mentioned, this blindness refers to the state of our lives before we know God as our savior. God's Word says that all of us have sinned and that our only source of redemption is through His Son Jesus Christ. However, if we confess our sins and accept Jesus as our Savior, we will be forgiven, and a new life will be ours.

Romans 3:23-24

...for all have sinned and fall short of the glory of God, and are justified by his grace as a gift, through the redemption that is in Christ Jesus...

VICTORY OVER SIN IS NOT ATTAINED THROUGH ANY EFFORT OF OURS, BUT ONLY THROUGH THE SHED BLOOD OF JESUS CHRIST.

John 3:16-18

For God so loved the world, that he gave his only Son, that whoever believes in him should not perish but have eternal life. For God did not send his Son into the world to condemn the world, but in order that the world might be saved through him. Whoever believes in him is not condemned, but whoever does not believe is condemned already, because he has not believed in the name of the only Son of God.

1 John 1:8-10

If we say we have no sin, we deceive ourselves, and the truth is not in us. If we confess our sins, he is faithful and just to forgive us our sins and to cleanse us from all unrighteousness. If we say we have not sinned, we make him a liar, and his word is not in us.

What more could we ask for than a faithful God who sacrificed His only Son to save us? This is a salvation that makes us heirs of God's kingdom and grants us eternal peace in our heavenly home, and a salvation that takes everything we accomplish and turns it into the glory of God for the purpose of His kingdom. Once again, that is one of the goals of this book—to help you know God more and assist you in developing a deeper relationship with Him and, furthermore, that you will become a vessel that He can use in mighty ways to impart hope, peace, and encouragement to others.

However, we must understand that victory over sin is not attained through any effort of ours, but only through the shed blood of Jesus Christ. It is only by God's grace and through the death and resurrection of His Son Jesus Christ that we have been redeemed from sin. It is only by God's power given to us through the Holy Spirit that we can overcome the power of the enemy.

Revelation 12:10–11

And I heard a loud voice in heaven, saying, "Now the salvation and the power and the kingdom of our God and the authority of his Christ have come, for the accuser of our brothers has been thrown down, who accuses them day and night before our God. And they have conquered him by the blood of the Lamb and by the word of their testimony, for they loved not their lives even unto death..."

I make this statement at the beginning of this book because the first chapter deals with the power and abilities of the enemy; he is called the Devil, Lucifer, or Satan—the father of all lies. However, God has overcome this enemy, and we must give all glory to Jesus Christ for that victory over sin and death.

Romans 1:2–4

...which he promised beforehand through his prophets in the holy Scriptures, concerning his Son, who was descended from David according to the flesh and was declared to be the Son of God in power according to the Spirit of holiness by his resurrection from the dead, Jesus Christ our Lord...

We must know that it is not in our power that we make war against evil, but by the power given to us through Jesus Christ.

Matthew 16:18–19

And I tell you, you are Peter, and on this rock I will build my church, and the gates of hell shall not prevail against it. I will give you the keys of the kingdom of heaven, and whatever you bind on earth shall be bound in heaven, and whatever you loose on earth shall be loosed in heaven.

Finally, it is the power given to us by God, as declared by Christ before He departed this earth that will carry us through the battles that we face.

Matthew 28:18–20

And Jesus came and said to them, "All authority in heaven and on earth has been given to me. Go therefore and make disciples of all nations, baptizing them in the name of the Father and of the Son and of the Holy Spirit, teaching them to observe all that I have commanded you. And behold, I am with you always, to the end of the age."

BATTLE PLAN

WE MUST

1. Accept that we were created to serve God, declare His greatness, minister in a lost world, and help others find the light of God.

2. Understand that this entire plan begins with our acceptance of Jesus Christ as Lord and Savior of our life.

3. Realize we are in God's Army and destined to become one of His great warriors.

4. Give our lives to God and be devoted to His path of forgiveness and righteousness.

If God is tugging at your heart, if your mind is racing with the thought that you need Jesus to help you, then He has prepared this exact moment in time for you to do so. You do not need to be in church or have a Pastor with you. All you need is a broken heart that is longing for something more than what this world can give, a heart that is searching for fulfillment and peace. You need Jesus.

Pray this with me: *Lord, today I come before You as one who has sinned. Father, I have not followed Your ways, and my desire today is to ask You to forgive me of my sins, cleanse my heart, and make me whole. Lord as You take that sin from my life, I ask that You fill me with Your Spirit and help me to follow the plan that You have for me. Give me the strength that I need to endure and grant me peace over the things that I have done against You. I ask this in the name of Jesus, believing that He is the resurrected Son of the living God. Amen.*

If you prayed this prayer today, from the depths of your heart, then you have been saved. Let me be the first to welcome you into the family of God and encourage you to let someone know about your decision. Understand, this is not the end of your salvation—it is only the beginning, and God has great things for you in the future. I would also ask that you please contact me or another believer and let me know of your decision, so that we may rejoice with you. It is also imperative that you plug into a local church or a Bible study so that you can be better equipped for the battles that you face. Now let's move forward in the plan God has for you.

In physical warfare, there are years of planning that take place before the first round is ever fired. We must plan for our attack and our defense. We must know our limitations and our strengths. We must also use our allies to our benefit and rely on other warriors to stand with us. None of us will ever succeed in a battle alone.

What plans do I need to make so that I can complete the specific missions that God has designed for me? (Exodus 19:5-6, Genesis 12:1-3)

How can I overcome the constant battle in my own mind, between my sinful nature and my desire, to pursue God? (Proverbs 3: 5-8)

In what ways can I share the faithfulness of God and the story of His Son's sacrifice for my salvation?

_____

_____

_____

_____

_____

_____

How can I mentor and help those who already know God to develop a deeper relationship with the King? (1 Peter 4:10, Colossians 3:16)

_____

_____

_____

_____

_____

_____

PRAYER:

Father in heaven, forgive me today of any uncaring attitude that I have had for others. Help me, beginning today, to seek You in new ways. Grant me the wisdom and boldness that I need to tell others about Your love. God, give me a new desire to serve You by serving others. Lord, please break my heart like Yours breaks for the lost and help me to love them with Your love, even the unlovable—for I too was once a sinner, and You saved my by Your grace. Lord, open up heaven and give me the grace that I need to see others in this world through Your eyes. Father, remind me each day of the declaration of Your Word that, "all authority in heaven and on earth has been given to me. Therefore I will go and make disciples of all nations, I will baptize them in the name of the

Father and of the Son and of the Holy Spirit, and I will teach them to obey everything You have commanded." Lord, I pray that Your Holy Spirit declares to my spirit each day that You are "with me always, even to the very end of the age." All of this I ask in the mighty name of Jesus the Christ. Amen.

THE ENEMY AND HIS TACTICS 3

A nother part of any battle we encounter is understanding our enemy. We must recognize their strengths, review their tactics, evaluate their available weapons, and prepare as much as possible for their attack or defense.

In this process, it is crucial that we do not underestimate the enemy's ability. Throughout the years, those who underestimated the ability and strength of those they fought have lost many battles; they underestimated the tenacity and commitment that their enemy possessed. For an enemy with great numbers of soldiers, it is many often their tactic to bring continual attacks until they wear down their stronger opponent through attrition.

These are the same aspects used in spiritual warfare. Therefore, we must take into account the enemies weapons, tactics, assets, strength, and commitment. In all of these areas, we know that the devil is already defeated by God through the death and resurrection of Jesus Christ. However, we must continually strive to become effective warriors for Christ as we engage in the fight against this enemy who seeks to destroy us. This is an essential part in the development of our attitude as a warrior for the kingdom of God. Furthermore, it is to this end that we will endeavor to understand against whom we are fighting.

The Word of God is clear when it describes to us the spiritual battle that we face.

Ephesians 6:12

For we do not wrestle against flesh and blood, but against the rulers, against the authorities, against the cosmic powers over this present darkness, against the spiritual forces of evil in the heavenly places.

37

John 10:10

The thief comes only to steal and kill and destroy. I came that they may have life and have it abundantly.

This Scripture describes our enemy the devil as a thief who comes only to steal, kill, and destroy. In this Scripture, the intentions of the enemy are plainly stated. It is the concept of a thief who is cunning in his attack, seeking those who are weak or unaware of his presence. He is a covert operator who hits his victims without warning then hides in the shadows awaiting another opportunity to inflict damage. He conceals his lies in partial truth so that it is easier to deceive us. For if he were to use them in a direct manner, they would be seen for what they truly are—lies. Therefore, do not expect a battle plan from the enemy that utilizes a direct attack. He will never walk in from the front to attack your position of strength. He will always implement a plan of attrition initiated by a coward that is used to break down and confuse the warrior and the bystander.

THE ENEMY CONCEALS HIS LIES IN PARTIAL TRUTH SO THAT IT IS EASIER TO DECEIVE US.

1 Peter 5:8–9

Be sober-minded; be watchful. Your adversary the devil prowls around like a roaring lion, seeking someone to devour. Resist him, firm in your faith, knowing that the same kinds of suffering are being experienced by your brotherhood throughout the world.

In this Scripture, the word sober-minded is used to describe someone who is serious and sensible. A person who is studious and logical. This should describe our efforts in this battle. Some versions of the Bible use the word vigilant in this passage. Webster's dictionary defines the word vigilant as "to keep watch or to stay awake, being alertly watchful especially to avoid danger." What better word could have been used to inform the warrior of his mission to always be aware of the danger that surrounds him, or to be fully aware and continuously watching for an enemy that will attack us when we least expect it?

Think about that for a moment. When you are on the battlefield you are looking all around for the enemy's attack. Where will he come from?

Is he behind a hill or a tree? Will he shoot form the house, jump out of a car or fire from a rooftop? Is the movement of tall grass caused by the wind or is my enemy crawling towards my position?

How will the attack occur? Will it be a mortar lobbed from a long distance or a suicide bomber walking up to my side? Will there be an RPG (rocket propelled grenade) fired at my vehicle or a belt fed machine gun throwing out hundreds of dangerous rounds in my direction? Will he use a secret group or attack me through a person I thought was my friend? Will it be a battle hardened warrior or a family member who ends my life?

We also have to look at the timing of an attack. Will the attack take place during the day or in the darkness of night? Is the enemy counting the number of team members in our group to calculate an advantage? Does he know when we are less in number due to our rotations and movements? Will he hit us when we are all sick and tired from our inhospitable surroundings?

Spiritually, we must be vigilant. Just like the one stationed in a combat zone, we must watch everything. The spiritual enemy of our soul can show up at any time, use any available cover, and employ any weapon at his disposal. Like one of my favorite Pastors used to say, "The devil is not crouching behind every rock…but he is behind every other rock."

Look again at the previous passage from 1 Peter 5:8. God uses the symbol of the lion to show that our enemy attacks in a ruthless and ferocious way. He uses the tactics of a predator as he waits in hiding to attack the weak and vulnerable, especially, those who stray from the flock and, thereby, relinquish their ability to be protected by the safety of numbers and the protection of the Shepherd. This is an enemy who does not approach us head on, but patiently stalks us until he finds an opportunity to catch us unaware. It is at that moment that he lunges at his prey to inflict his deadly strike.

Think about the times that you are vulnerable to that type of attack. We may be dealing with the loss of a job, a death in the family, or some other difficult event. During that time, we can be overcome with feelings of despair and frustration. The enemy will use this challenging time to interject his lies. He may begin by saying that God made that situation happen because you had not obeyed His divine will. Another one of his favorite lies is that God did not hear your prayers for help during the trial that you faced. He even tells us that God does not care, or that God does not even exist. These are the types of things the devil uses to distort the truth.

Yet we are not to live in fear of this enemy, for we know that God has provided a way for our salvation. It is through His divine intervention that we can walk upright and sure throughout life, knowing that we are protected by the hand of the Almighty God from all evil. Through the death and resurrection of Jesus Christ, the Son of God, we are redeemed from the bondage of sin and eternal death. We become heirs with Christ to an eternal life with our faithful God. Furthermore, it was Christ's victory over sin and the grave that gives us the power to overcome our enemy and the evil that rules this world.

As we continue to define our enemy, we look at the parable of the tares found in Matthew 13. This Scripture speaks of the enemy that attacks in the night. It describes the kingdom of heaven, which is like a man who plants good seed in his field. Yet, while the men and his servants slept, his enemy came and planted weeds among the wheat, then went away. As the story continues, the wheat begins to grow, but with it comes the weeds to choke out new life.

THE ENEMY IS AN OPPORTUNIST. IF WE LET OUR GUARD DOWN FOR ONLY A MOMENT, HE WILL SNEAK IN AND PLANT HIS EVIL DEVICES.

Therefore, we must recognize that the enemy is an opportunist. If we let our guard down for only a moment, he will sneak in and plant his evil devices, some of which may not sprout until a later time. However, because we were unable to distinguish the good seeds from the bad, they will grow with the potential for destruction. We can only resolve this issue by carefully tending the crop and monitoring its growth.

Here is a spiritual fact of life: We all have, what we call, little sins that we ignore. They are things that we know are wrong, but do not see how they affect our lives or the lives of those around us, things that lurk in the deepest crevice of our souls. These sins appear to be trivial, so we ignore their existence as we compromise our walk with Christ. These weeds, left unchecked however, can grow until they choke life out of the good seeds that have been planted. As the good seed dies, we become defeated in our spirit as more stumbling blocks develop. Eventually, they will not only affect us but also our families, friends, and those who God has placed in our path. Only our decision to follow God's divine will and His perfect ways will take us past the snares that await us; and move us into a conscious and committed walk with God. Therefore, we must admit our faults to God, ask for forgiveness, and then move forward in His grace. Remember: Ignoring our little issues will not make them go away. Deal with them today and ask God to help you know the best way to avoid the temptation in the future.

What weeds are growing in your field? Do you have a problem with lying? Are your lips filled with gossip? Or like the children of Israel, do you constantly gripe and complain about everything around you? Remember that critical spirit forced them to walk around the desert for forty years until they died, never entering into the land promised by God.

Those little weeds can have a huge negative effect on our future and perhaps even our eternity. Stop and pray now, so that God can remove those weeds before they grow any stronger.

BATTLE PLAN

WE MUST

1. Be aware of the spiritual dangers that surround our lives.

2. Prepare daily to enter into the combat zone.

3. Study God's Word to know what weapons of God are available to help us in the battle. (Read the spiritual warfare prayer again at the beginning of this book.)

4. Begin each day in prayer and pray continually for God to reveal the danger of sin that pursues us. These temptations surround each person daily, but God will give us the strength to overcome their destructive power.

SPIRITUAL EXERCISE NOTE: IN THE MORNINGS, GO THROUGH THE ARMOR OF GOD.

Put on your shirt or blouse as you pray over the Breastplate of Righteousness that covers your heart that day. Consciously ask God to help you love the unlovable and seek His peace in all situations.

As you tighten your belt, allow God to use the Belt of Truth to expose the lies that you will face that day, lies of the enemy that tell you that you have no value. On the contrary, believe God's truth that you are so valuable that He sacrificed His Son for your eternal life.

As you comb or brush your hair, put on a hat, or your glasses thank God for His Helmet of Salvation, the salvation that has saved you from sin and has promise you eternal peace with God in heaven.

When you put on your shoes, know that you have been prepared by God to carry the Gospel of Peace to those who cross your path. In addition to Him preparing you, He has also gone before you to prepare the hearts of the people you will encounter that day so that you may plant the seed of His message into their lives.

As you walk through your day, thank God for the Shield of Faith that He has given you, faith to move mountains and protect you from the attacks of the enemy. Also know that your faith is working even when there is no physical evidence of its effect, faith that spurs you on with hope for the things God will do in and through your life.

As you go through this process, know that you have begun your day with the Sword of the Spirit, which is the Word of God. Your initial effort in enabling the power of God was to acknowledge Him at the beginning of the day. Then you established His Word in your life by quoting the very purpose of His armor. Finally, by thanking God and acknowledging the work of Christ on the cross for your salvation, you have submitted yourself to Him. This cognitive and spiritual process has equipped you for the day. You can now move forward knowing that every part of your life is in the very hand of God; therefore, He will protect you, provide for you, and direct you in every step of the day.

Now move out, warrior. Your victory is secured through the blood of Jesus Christ, the work of the Holy Spirit, and the Word of God.

DEVOTIONAL

In this chapter, I have explained the importance of understanding the tactics of our enemy. This includes the ways he attacks us and the types of weapons that he utilizes.

In what ways does the enemy attack me?

_____

_____

_____

_____

_____

How have I seen him attack others?

_____

_____

_____

_____

_____

How can I become more aware of the enemy, who seeks to steal my joy, kill my desire, and destroy my walk with God? (Luke 21:36, 1 Peter 1:13)

_____

_____

_____

_____

How can I help protect my family and others from those same attacks?
(Psalm 5:1–12)

_____

_____

_____

_____

How can I become more self-controlled, so that I do not waver in
battle? (Titus 1:8–9)

_____

_____

_____

_____

What habitual sins are in my life that may give the enemy more opportunity to attack my position?

_____

_____

_____

_____

PRAYER:

Lord, help me to always be aware of the enemy around me. Give me
discernment to recognize his attacks. Father, forgive me of the sins I
have committed against You and help me to remain diligent as I flee
from the temptations that surround me. Jesus, thank you for the work
You accomplished on the cross to sanctify my life. Amen.

OUR ENEMY IS A TERRORIST

4

As we define our enemy, we can use a title that has come to the forefront of our world in recent years. The devil is a terrorist. This is a great word to use when describing the work of the devil and tactics that he employs. You see, a terrorist uses manipulation, deceit, coercion, and covert tactics to reach his goals. He does so by oppressing, restraining, dominating, or destroying his victims. He uses force to compel them as he unleashes his acts of violence and destruction upon those who are innocent or unaware.

As we have witnessed, acts of terrorism are rarely carried out in a face-to-face confrontation. A terrorist in all actuality is the ultimate coward, hiding behind women and children to carry out their destruction. They will even use their own family as a shield to fulfill their mission. Just as the devil uses innocent and unknowing victims to carry out his evil plans, ultimately resulting in their destruction. He is not concerned with their well-being, only with the evil goal of his plan to destroy all things.

To understand the terrorist concept, I will explain some facts about terrorists and their efforts. This is done so that we can become more aware of the subtle ways that the devil seeks to use others to destroy us. The stories below are real events that will reveal a dark world that most of us are unaware exists; that in itself is another reason for the stories. Many of us are unaware of the existence of spiritual warfare. However, our lack of knowledge in that subject does not mean that it is not affecting our lives and the lives of those around us. Please understand that these stories are not meant to offend. I have even left out many detailed facts for those who may think that it is more information than they want to know, but these are perfect examples of how covert acts, innocent victims, and unusual circumstances can be used by our earthly and our spiritual enemies.

Here are some examples of real terrorist operations:

As a military convoy moves through an Afghan village, they observe a seven to nine-year-old boy walk towards the approaching vehicles. As he gets to within a few yards, his small body explodes resulting in his death and injury to others in the immediate area. An investigation into the incident reveals that the boy's father (a follower of Islam dedicated to jihad {holy war}), has wrapped his son's body with explosives and detonated the charge when he was in range of the convoy. The father, several hundred feet from the explosion had initiated the violent event by calling the cell phone that was attached to the boy's detonator. This father's cowardly effort was focused on the destruction of the convoy. His concern about his son was non-existent, unlike his desire to do harm to others. His dark soul overcame his natural instinct to care for his own child.

In a separate event, terrorists used women to infiltrate military bases. Knowing that the men would be searched at the entry gate of the base, it was decided that women would be used instead. Knowing that women in the Muslim world cannot be touched by another man that is not related to them, the plan was to take advantage of a religious practice, a practice that made it a violation to search a woman approaching the guard gate. To implement the plan, terrorists located women who had been rejected by Islam and their society for a variety of reasons. They had no hope of entering the heavens of Islam unless they carried out a desperate act in the name of their god, Allah. These poor victims were then wrapped in explosives and sent into the military facilities. If allowed in the base or near the facility, the charges were then initiated by other terrorists in the area by sending an electronic signal to the charge.

Finally, I will share a story that I heard directly from the victims involved in the act. While working in a small village (not named to protect the innocent), I saw an opportunity to assist a local orphanage. This orphanage was filled with boys and girls between the ages of six and seventeen. During one of my visits, I noticed a young man who was walking with crutches and was missing one leg. When I asked him how he lost his leg, he told me his heart-wrenching story:

One day while walking in his village, the Taliban came to seek refuge and obtain the things that they needed to continue their fight. One need that they had involved the clearing of a minefield in the area. These fields are common throughout the country and many have been there for years, since the Russian occupation. To clear the field, the Taliban ordered the children of the village to walk through the minefield. When they refused and the parents began to plead with them, they started shooting the people in the village. Therefore, the children were compelled by fear, to make the harrowing walk. On that day, many of them would not leave the field alive. The young boy (age 12) that told me the story, had stepped on a mine and lost his leg. Fortunately, he was found by passing military personnel and taken to a field hospital, where his life was saved. Unfortunately, his sister and the rest of his family died, and he was left alone to fend for himself. He was brought to the orphanage I had helped develop, where he still lives today and is receiving a positive Christian influence in his life.

I know that these accounts are hard to read, and for Westerners not exposed to these terrible acts, are very difficult to believe. However, there are countless incidents like these that can be confirmed by military personnel throughout the world. In the same way, spiritual warfare and the evil ways of the devil are hard to believe. There are even those out there who will scoff at the idea of spiritual warfare or that the devil exists, but the facts are made clear in Scripture and the results of destruction that we see in Afghanistan, Iraq, Africa, Mexico, North America, and many other places throughout the world should be proof enough that evil does exist and the devil is real.

So how does the devil use these covert tactics against us? The answer is this: many times he uses subtle devices to undermine the work of God. This may begin with little white lies, gossip about our friends, arguments between believers, berating a Pastor behind his back, or an innocent peek at a pornographic site on the Internet. These small events can create a sense of shame or defeat in our lives. If we do not deal with those sins, they become a foothold that the devil can use to cultivate additional guilt and lead us into deeper and more dangerous sins.

Ephesians 4:25–32

Therefore, having put away falsehood, let each one of you speak the truth with his neighbor, for we are members one of another. Be angry and do not sin; do not let the sun go down on your anger, and give no opportunity to the devil. Let the thief no longer steal, but rather let him labor, doing honest work with his own hands, so that he may have something to share with anyone in need. Let no corrupting talk come out of your mouths, but only such as is good for building up, as fits the occasion, that it may give grace to those who hear. And do not grieve the Holy Spirit of God, by whom you were sealed for the day of redemption. Let all bitterness and wrath and anger and clamor and slander be put away from you, along with all malice. Be kind to one another, tenderhearted, forgiving one another, as God in Christ forgave you.

Each time we sin in these ways, we create further separation from God. We build up more shame, and it begins to envelop our lives. It steals our joy as we accept the devalued state in which we are living. All the while, the enemy continues his oppression by reminding us of our worthless state.

The devil may also use our position of authority or the work that we do for God as a trap. He begins to allow the praises we receive from others to increase our ego. If that haughty spirit goes unchecked, it can develop into sin that undermines God's glory, and can even have a negative result on the effectiveness of the ministry effort.

1 Peter 5:2–7

...shepherd the flock of God that is among you, exercising oversight, not under compulsion, but willingly, as God would have you; not for shameful gain, but eagerly; not domineering over those in your charge, but being examples to the flock. And when the chief Shepherd appears, you will receive the unfading crown of glory. Likewise, you who are younger, be subject to the elders. Clothe yourselves, all of you, with humility toward one another, for "God opposes the proud but gives grace to the humble." Humble yourselves, therefore, under the mighty hand of God so that at the proper time he may exalt you, casting all your anxieties on him, because he cares for you.

These examples are just some of the ways we can be attacked. If we become lazy in our ways, it opens us to a stagnated walk with Jesus. We stop reading our Bible, move away from our Christian relationships, stop going to church, and separate ourselves from the things of God. By increasing our distance from the protection of God, the enemy can sneak in and plant small, inconspicuous minefields. Dangerous traps that are strategically placed along a path that intersects with the direction of our mission for God. These little charges may remain in place for years; then one day when we step a little bit too far from the path set by God, and we trigger the devastating blast. When we walk into these areas that have been declared off limits by God, the devil ignites a charge that can undermine our relationship with God.

However, there is something about these mine fields that we must know. Mine fields in and of themselves are not always meant to completely destroy. They are typically used to slow the advancement of troops, create a sense of fear, and incapacitate or distract the warriors from their mission. They are also used to deplete our resources by affecting those in battle around us. This occurs when one soldier steps on a mine and becomes injured. It now takes a medic to provide care and other soldiers to remove him from the danger area and back to safety. This depletes our battle unit and creates another gap in the line of security that we rely upon.

FOR IT IS THE PROTECTION OF GOD, THE SACRIFICIAL BLOOD OF CHRIST, AND THE OVERWHELMING POWER OF THE HOLY SPIRIT THAT MAKE US VICTORIOUS WARRIORS.

Are these tactics and weapons that we can avoid? Yes. However, since this is a spiritual battle we must recognize that attempting to stand against Satan in our own power, we are doomed. Our enemy, the devil, is a powerful adversary that has more than enough strength to defeat mortal man; however, when his war is waged against a faithful and obedient child of almighty God, his efforts become fruitless, for it is the protection of God, the sacrificial blood of Christ, and the overwhelming power of the Holy Spirit that make us victorious warriors over all things. Therefore, we do not stand in our own power, but under the power and authority given to us through Jesus Christ.

Ephesians 1:18–23

...having the eyes of your hearts enlightened, that you may know what is the hope to which he has called you, what are the riches of his glorious inheritance in the saints, and what is the immeasurable greatness of his power toward us who believe, according to the working of his great might that he worked in Christ when he raised him from the dead and seated him at his right hand in the heavenly places, far above all rule and authority and power and dominion, and above every name that is named, not only in this age but also in the one to come. And he put all things under his feet and gave him as head over all things to the church, which is his body, the fullness of him who fills all in all.

BATTLE PLAN

WE MUST

1. Move forward trusting God for all things as we strive to fight the battle that lies before us. Learn to rely on His strength and provision.

2. Pray for the protection of our families, our friends, and ourselves. Scripture tells us to pray unceasingly and to pray for all the saints. Prayer is power and gives us a direct connection to God.

3. Trust God for His divine intervention. We cannot fight the battle in our own power. Plus, when we submit to God and rely on Him, He blesses our humility and submission with divine protection and provision.

4. Keep our eyes on Jesus. Whenever we look to other sources for our strength, we will ultimately be defeated. However, if we continually look to God for His help, we are promised victory.

I spoke of the enemy as a terrorist. He is one who manipulates and attacks the weak. He also promotes fear and plants confusion in our hearts and minds. He is the ultimate deceiver looking to oppress everyone he sees. I went on to define the weak as those who are innocent of his ways or unaware of his existence.

In what ways can I assist other believers in overcoming the enemy?

_____

_____

_____

_____

_____

_____

What are some ways that I can be victorious over Satan according to Philippians 4:6–9?

_____

_____

_____

_____

_____

_____

_____

How can my words and actions be used by the enemy? What steps can I take to keep that from happening?

_____

_____

_____

_____

_____

_____

How does bitterness, rage, slander, malice, negative attitudes or unwholesome talk infect my life? (Define them)

_____

_____

_____

_____

_____

If these things are present, what can I do to allow God to purge them from my life? (2 Timothy 2:21)

_____

_____

_____

_____

_____

Note: I know that it is hard to think about the shameful things that we do. I also know that it is easy to hide them from the people around us. However, the things in our life that are not pleasing to God create a foothold for the enemy to launch progressively lethal attacks. The longer we hold on to our sin and deny or cover up its existence, the more it can create a greater separation between God and us. It causes us to build up more shame, waters the seeds of guilt, and eventually envelops our lives. It steals our joy and allows the devil to devalue our position in Christ. All the while, the enemy uses it to bring oppression and depression into our heart and mind.

PRAYER:

Lord, I ask You to cleanse me of sin and accept the divine fact that I am a wonderfully made child of God. Help to see the value that You have given to me through the sacrifice of Your Son for my salvation, sanctification, and healing. Lord, help me to walk everyday like the child of God that I am in You.

WEAPONS THAT DESTROY

5

A s we have discussed, it is crucial that we understand our enemy in this battle. Therefore, it is also crucial that we identify some of the specific weapons and tactics that he uses against us. By identifying these areas of attack, we will more clearly see how he attempts to defeat us, thereby preparing us to defend ourselves from his destructive ways.

Before listing these weapons, I want to make clear that there are many other weapons than those mentioned here that the devil could use to attack us; to mention each one would take volumes of discussion on the subject. Therefore, I will only mention a few so that we can see how they are used by the enemy in his effort to destroy mankind and especially the followers of God.

Our relationship with God is the one thing that our enemy hates the most, and he knows that undermining our daily relationship with God is the key to our destruction. He also knows that it is this divine relationship through Jesus Christ that allows us to have power over his evil plans. Therefore, if he can disrupt our relationship with God, he can move about more freely in our lives.

This tactic is shown initially in the fall of man from God's grace through Adam. In Genesis 3, the Bible says that Adam took the fruit that was declared off limits by God and ate it. At that moment, Adam's eyes were opened to his sin against God, and he hid from God. This became man's first separation from his creator and the act of sin that allowed evil to find its way into man's heart and into the world. It is this evil that separates us from a relationship with God, as our disobedient nature keeps us from proper communication and relationship with Him.

Just like Adam and Eve, when we sin, we run from God in an attempt to escape the conviction of His holy presence. When hiding doesn't work to appease our guilt and shame, we then attempt to justify our actions by fabricating reasons and excuses for our sinful deeds. This is exactly what Satan wants because he knows that as we find ways to defend our actions, we create a wider gap between our sinfulness and the restorative nature of God.

WHEN WE COMMIT SIN, WE NEED TO RUN IMMEDIATELY INTO THE LOVING ARMS OF OUR HEAVENLY FATHER.

We need to understand that God's convicting power is not there to destroy us. On the contrary, it is His tender loving conviction that is an essential element of God's guiding hand. It is the tool that He uses to keep us in check and to direct us away from sin. Without this spiritual intervention, our sinful nature would cause us to pursue sin in such a way that it would result in our ultimate and eternal destruction. Remember, Jesus said that He came to save us, not condemn us. His only desire for us is a more abundant life and an eternal future filled with His glorious presence.

John 10:10-11

The thief comes only to steal and kill and destroy. I came that they may have life and have it abundantly. I am the good shepherd. The good shepherd lays down his life for the sheep.

That is why we need to train ourselves in the art of spiritual restoration. When we commit sin, we need to run immediately into the loving arms of our heavenly Father. It is there where we will find comfort and peace. It is in His arms that we will receive a fullness in life that nothing else can give. Yes, there may be a price to pay for our disobedience, but the price we pay for our actions will be very small compared to the cost of continued defiance and the risk of eternal separation from God.

Let us look a little further into the restorative ways of God through the character of King David. In the many stories told about his life, we see him crying out to God for the sins he has committed. He is passionate about living for God, but a slave to the sinful nature that lives within him. Like David, we too have this constant internal battle, as we succumb to the pressures of our inner man, but David recognized his weakness and continually expressed it to his heavenly Father in verse and in song, a cry of the heart that sought forgiveness and righteousness above all things. We see an example of this in a few verses from Psalm 51:

Psalm 51:1–3 & 10–12

Have mercy on me, O God, according to your steadfast love; according to your abundant mercy blot out my transgressions. Wash me thoroughly from my iniquity, and cleanse me from my sin! For I know my transgressions, and my sin is ever before me...Create in me a clean heart, O God, and renew a right spirit within me. Cast me not away from your presence, and take not your Holy Spirit from me. Restore to me the joy of your salvation, and uphold me with a willing spirit.

Like David, when we cry out to God, He responds in an amazing way. In David's case, this willingness to run back to God after his sinful acts led the Holy Spirit to inspire Luke to write these words:

Acts 13:22

And when he had removed him, he raised up David to be their king, of whom he testified and said, "I have found in David the son of Jesse a man after my heart, who will do all my will."

Can you imagine the God of the universe declaring that you are a man after His own heart? What a testimony of David's heart and desire to serve God, a desire to live pure and blameless even though he knew that sin crouched at his door. What a statement of faith by David to continually run after God even in the midst of his troubles. Oh, that we would run after God with that sort of devotion. What a great blessing we would be if we sought Him out in a greater way even though we are sinful creatures.

We see this recognition of sin again in the life of the disciple Peter. He and his friends are fishing, and Jesus performs a miracle causing them to catch an abundance of fish. When Peter recognizes that he is in the very presence of the Messiah, he falls to his knees and cries out in submission:

Luke 5:8

But when Simon Peter saw it, he fell down at Jesus' knees, saying, "Depart from me, for I am a sinful man, O Lord."

When we see our sin like Peter saw his, Jesus does not run from us, but runs towards us with His arms open wide! It is this humbling of the heart that allows God to work in and through us. It opens us up to God's refreshing power and allows Him to bring restoration to our very soul. Once restored into His righteousness, He can then empower us to bear godly fruit to the glory of His name.

In reality, an attitude of repentance delivers us from the captivity of our sin and restores our heart to a right relationship with God, a relationship that promises to give rest to our weary heart and refresh our spirit in a new way, thereby removing the burden of guilt and shame so that we can escape the darkness that sin creates within us.

Jeremiah 31:25

For I will satisfy the weary soul, and every languishing soul I will replenish.

This concept goes along with one of my favorite passages in the Bible. It is found in Jeremiah, and if you read it closely you will see the power of seeking God in every situation.

Jeremiah 29:11–14

For I know the plans I have for you, declares the Lord, plans for welfare and not for evil, to give you a future and a hope. Then you will call upon me and come and pray to me, and I will hear you. You will seek me and find me, when you seek me with all your heart. I will be found by you, declares the Lord, and I will restore your fortunes and gather you from all the nations and all the places where I have driven you, declares the Lord, and I will bring you back to the place from which I sent you into exile.

BATTLE PLAN

WE MUST

1. Go to God when we have been disobedient to Him. David was called a man after God's own heart because he always turned back to God when he sinned. Therefore, when conviction comes our way, do not run away from God like Adam and Eve. Instead, run to God and into His living arms.

2. Seek righteousness daily. It is not hard for us to sin because that is in our human nature. Therefore, we must continually evaluate our lives to be sure we are walking in the right direction, looking to the things of God to give us encouragement and purpose in life.

3. Value our relationship with God above all things. We can do this by putting God first in our marriage, in our relationships, in our work, in our families, etc. God never wants us to set aside our responsibilities to serve Him. What He actually desires is for us to work in and through His presence in every aspect of our lives. If we put God into everything, then His plan will come together in and through us each day. A plan that is always a win-win-win scenario. If we do things God's way, a) we win, b) others win and c) and the kingdom of God wins. What better things could we ask for in life?

We have already discussed the enemy in this battle. Therefore, we do not want to give him any additional credit. However, let's look at how God can overpower the weapons the enemy uses against us.

In what ways does guilt define and undermine my life?

_____

_____

_____

_____

_____

The definition of conviction from *Christian Apologetics & Research Ministry*:

> *Conviction* is the work of the Holy Spirit where a person is able to see himself as God sees him: guilty, defiled, and totally unable to save himself (John 16:8). Conviction for the non-Christian, reveals sinfulness, guilt, and brings fear of God's righteous judgment. Conviction in the believer brings an awareness of sin and results in repentance, confession and cleansing.

How does God use conviction to restore my relationship with Him?

_____

_____

_____

_____

What convictions has God revealed in my life that I have failed to turn over to Him?

_____

_____

_____

_____

_____

What can I do to shed that conviction? (2 Kings 22:19)

_____

_____

_____

_____

How do I continually pursue the righteousness of God? (2 Timothy 2:22, Isaiah 51:1)

_____

_____

_____

_____

Remember: Guilt can be used by God to lead us back to conviction and redemption. However, most guilt comes from our own condemnation or the condemnation of others. Therefore, the negative guilt that you may sense is not always something used by God. Let me explain it this way: That negative guilt that you or others put on you comes from the devil; he may even use guilt against you to make you fall into a progressive state of depression. That is why I believe that almost all guilt comes directly from the devil himself. Why? Guilt places you in a downward spiral that you cannot escape.

Conviction on the other hand (which comes from God), leads you back into His loving arms and saving grace. When God convicts, He always gives us an opportunity to repent.

Here is an analogy that I use: Guilt is like a dog chasing his tail. He goes around and around and around. He uses up all kinds of energy, but never really accomplishes anything. In fact, he can get so involved in chasing his tail that you can walk right past him, and he won't even see you go by.

You see, the ring of guilt uses up your energy and makes you ineffective in the work that God has called you to accomplish. So when you sense guilt, stop and pray to determine whether it is true conviction or just the type of guilt from the enemy that is going to run you in circles. If it is not from God, ask Him to intervene on your behalf so the devil will leave you alone. However, if it is conviction, run as fast as you can back to God and ask Him to forgive you. Does that make sense? Then do it, because God only wants to bring restoration into your life.

FRIENDLY FIRE

his section is one of the most important in this book and may bring about some negative statements from believers. However, it is time that we address this major issue in the Christian world.

As stated previously, casualties are sometimes caused by a thing known as "friendly fire." This applies to physical and spiritual warfare. Wikipedia defines friendly fire as:

> Friendly fire is often seen as an inescapable result of combat, and because it accounts for a small percentage (estimated 2% to, rarely, as high as 20%) of casualties, can often be dismissed as irrelevant to the outcome of a battle. The effects of friendly fire, however, are not just material. Troops expect to be targeted by the enemy, but being hit by their own forces has a huge negative impact on morale. Forces doubt the competence of their command, and its prevalence makes commanders more cautious in the field. Attempts to reduce this effect by military leaders generally come down to identifying the causes of friendly fire and overcoming repetition of the incident through training, tactics and technology.

Now let's look at examples of friendly fire in worldwide combat actions, reported by the pages of history. The following examples were taken from: *Wikipedia, the free encyclopedia, "Friendly Fire." Last updated March 29, 2016. https://en.wikipedia.org/wiki/ List_of_friendly_fire_incidents (4-1-16).*

FRENCH AND INDIAN WAR

This friendly fire incident was blamed on poor training and lack of discipline.

Two main phases of friendly fire occurred during the Battle of the Monongahela, which halted the Braddock Expedition of British regular "redcoat" and British American colonial troops after a combined force of French regulars, French-Canadian militia and allied Native Americans joined battle with them before Fort Duquesne. In the obscuring woodland conditions and confusion caused by the French musket fire and the Native Americans' war cries, several redcoat platoons fired at each other. Later in the battle many American colonials, lacking the redcoats' training in standing their ground, fled from more exposed ground and into woods, where redcoats fired on them mistaking them for advancing French fighters.

AMERICAN REVOLUTIONARY WAR

In the Battle of Guilford Courthouse on March 15, 1781, after several volleys of musket and cannon fire between American and British troops, smoke began to obscure soldiers' view of the battlefield. In a pitched battle, smoke not only limited visibility but irritated soldiers' eyes and could make breathing difficult. In the confusion, British Lieutenant John Macleod, in command of two British three-pounders, was directed by British Lieutenant General Charles Cornwallis to fire on the Americans and the British alike. Many British soldiers died as a result of friendly artillery bombardment.

AMERICAN CIVIL WAR

During the Battle of Antietam on 17 September 1862, a Confederate regiment had maneuvered into a gap between two Union regiments, the 9th New York and the 5th Massachusetts. The Confederates launched a surprise attack during a Union advance into the west woods. The 9th New York hastily began returning fire and unknowingly hit the 5th Massachusetts with musket fire that overshot the Confederate regiment, causing the other Union regiment to return fire in confusion. The two Union regiments had sustained heavy casualties during the lengthy exchange of fire. This was one of 11 friendly fire events recorded at Antietam, which taken together, were thought to have accounted for 1,150 killed and wounded, or approximately 5% of the total casualties.

WORLD WAR I

At night in foul weather on 16 September 1917, the British submarine HMS G9 mistook the destroyer HMS Pasley for a German U-boat and attacked with torpedoes. Pasley, not recognizing G9 as British until too late, responded to the attack by ramming G9. Nearly cut in two, the G9 sank. Only one of the G9's crew members survived.

It has been estimated that there may have been as many as 8,000 friendly fire incidents in the Vietnam War; one was the inspiration for the book and 1979 film, *Friendly Fire*.

> 19 November 1967, a U.S. Marine Corps. F4 Phantom aircraft dropped a 500 lb (230 kg) bomb on the command post of the 2nd Battalion (Airborne) 503rd Infantry, 173rd Airborne Brigade while they were in heavy contact with a numerically superior NVA force. At least 45 paratroopers were killed and another 45 wounded. Also killed was the Battalion Chaplain Major Charles J. Watters, who was subsequently awarded the Medal of Honor.

These stories of friendly fire go on and on. In many cases, the friendly fire is caused in physical battles by fatigue, poor vision, misunderstood objectives, misinterpretation of the situation, lack of discipline or training, poor command structure, and a variety of other contributing factors.

Whatever the cause, friendly fire is an accidental self-inflicted destruction of our own people. Personally, I see this as one of the most terrible ways to lose lives. To aggravate the loss, we find that these casualties are typically inflicted based on the loss of three very important components—communication, competent leadership, and obedience to commands.

When we lose proper communication with our command post or our support units we are heading for problems. As the minute details of the conflict are misunderstood, they can become major components to the breakdown of the mission. This breakdown causes us to fail in completing the mission, as we are unable to fulfill the orders that were issued. It is not that these orders were wrong. In fact, most of these orders were written based on real time information from forward observation posts with actual eyes on the enemy; they were detailed facts that would allow a direct mission to fully succeed. Unfortunately, in any battle, you can only prepare for known or speculated situations. Therefore, it is impossible to cover every possible action or circumstance that may be presented by the enemy.

In addition to the lack of proper communication, the incompetence of leadership can have a major impact on the task at hand. To say that a unit is only as good as its leaders is very true. Unfortunately, many choose their leaders based on charisma, longevity, or personal

connections instead of character, integrity, and ability. In our business-
es, governments, armies, and other organized groups throughout the
world, many key positions are filled with people who advance through
longevity and not ability. They move through the ranks because they
know someone, are related to an influential person, or have schmoozed
their way into a position.

OUR MISSION IS COMPROMISED WHEN WE FAIL TO FAITHFULLY FOLLOW THE COMMANDS WE ARE GIVEN.

Finally, in physical battle, our mission is compromised when we fail
to faithfully follow the commands we are given. Our standard operating
procedures require that we not only listen to the commands, but also
execute them as directed. When we fail to properly execute our orders
in a mission, we endanger our comrades, the innocent bystanders, and
ourselves in our area of operations.

However, those factors are not limited only to physical battle. When we
are in the midst of spiritual battle, the same factors can occur. When they
do, the spiritual casualties are much more difficult to determine. However,
the scope of loss can be great, and the damage done is still attributed to
the friendly fire that is encountered.

What causes these spiritual friendly fire incidents to occur? In some
cases, it may be incompetent spiritual leadership. These leaders that
are placed in positions that they are not qualified to hold. This is especially true when someone takes a position based on money or other
worldly factors instead of following God to the specific place they
were called.

This incompetence can also occur when a leader stretches his authority beyond the boundaries that have been established by God for his
position. We see this in the case of King Saul, Israel's first king. The
initial error in this process was the people wanting a king like their idol
worshiping neighbors, a king that in reality would replace God as their
sovereign leader. God even told them that this king would require great
things from them and warned the people that when they cried to Him
later for relief, He would not answer their cries. In the end, Saul would
bring about his own demise for his lack of obedience to God and his
unwillingness to follow directions.

Friendly fire can also occur when we develop poor spiritual attitudes. These are lackadaisical and unconcerned thoughts about the things of God. Sometimes we fall into a religious rut and begin to believe our own theologies over the truth of God's Word. This occurs when we fail to gain the biblical training and understanding that is needed to survive the conflicts that we face. This lack of training and discipline in spiritual things causes us to use our spiritual weapons improperly, sometimes discharging ineffective rounds in an attempt to help those around us. A misdirected barrage that is ineffective against the enemy and, in some cases, destroys the very people we have been sent to help. Friendly fire causes our family, friends, and neighbors to become casualties of the spiritual battle that surrounds us.

While we are on this subject, let's deal with one of the major factors affecting the church today. It is the lack of cooperation and Christian love. This lack of love not only creates casualties, but also brings about conflict in virtually every church in America. I will explain just a few of the incidents that I have seen, or been told of by others, during my time in the church as a member and as a leader. (These examples have been kept generic so as not to offend the guilty parties).

Hang on this may step on a few toes, but it is a time to deal with facts and not sweep our dirt under the carpet...please bear with me.

EXAMPLE 1

A longtime member is approached by a new believer/adherent of the church who wants to help during church functions. Unbeknownst to this new person, the longtime member they have approached is the self-proclaimed provider of all social activities in the church. This is "their" church and "they" are the only ones who can handle the things that occur in this little kingdom, a place where "they" have worked tirelessly for over 40 years and have never (in "their" opinion) been given one ounce of thanks for "their" tireless and selfless efforts.

As the new believer attempts to get involved in ministry by volunteering for church functions, the longtime member becomes irritated and begins a course of verbal abuse against the new member. Somehow, the new believers desire to get involved has stepped on the toes of the longtime ruler of this little part of the kingdom and has been met with an onslaught of trouble. The sad thing is the new person had no intention of creating conflict. They merely wanted to get involved and do their part to assist their new church friends any way that they could.

How does the enemy use this scenario? He helps "them" (little kingdom builders) become a little deity in "their" own eyes. "Their" years of experience and "their" obviously superior spiritual maturity make "them" the only ones who can do anything right, anywhere in the church. Unfortunately, "they" have been completely blinded by the opportunity that "they" have been given to mentor others and help the new believer/adherent become an integral part of the church family. A better approach would have been to encourage the new person to be involved and welcome them into this family of believers. When we drive people away from the area we have claimed to be our own, we drive them away from positive influence, good relationships and, sometimes, drive them right out of the church. Shame on us for thinking that we own the things of God and the church that He has built.

EXAMPLE 2

This story comes from the story of Job. Job, a man faultless in the eyes of God, is pelted with trouble and adversity of every kind. He loses his family, his servants, and his animals. He becomes inflicted with disease and does all that he can to give God glory for His sovereignty and power.

In this story, we also see Job's so-called "friends." Here are his buddies in the midst of his suffering, standing by to give him advice. Did they pray for him? Did they try to resolve his problems? Did they even go to the farm to see what was going on? No! All they did was sit around, giving him their tremendous wisdom to help him through his ordeal.

Job 2:11–13

Now when Job's three friends heard of all this evil that had come upon him, they came each from his own place, Eliphaz the Temanite, Bildad the Shuhite, and Zophar the Naamathite. They made an appointment together to come to show him sympathy and comfort him. And when they saw him from a distance, they did not recognize him. And they raised their voices and wept, and they tore their robes and sprinkled dust on their heads toward heaven. And they sat with him on the ground seven days and seven nights, and no one spoke a word to him, for they saw that his suffering was very great.

Sympathize and comfort him? Are you kidding me? They sat around and felt sorry for him—probably thinking that they were glad it wasn't

UNLESS YOU HAVE TRULY HEARD FROM GOD, IT MAY BE BEST TO KEEP YOUR MOUTH CLOSED.

happening to them. This kind of help is always available in the church. As you walk down a path of pain and suffering, here comes somebody at church to throw Scriptures at you. He knows nothing about your situation and has never asked you how you are doing or what's going on. In reality, the person of this world just enjoys hearing air moving through their mouth, and they don't actually hear the words they are saying. Just for reference: this is not helpful. Furthermore, it is far from being Christian. Christianity is based on love and relationship. Therefore, unless you have truly heard from God, it may be best to keep your mouth closed.

These examples and thoughts are not made to discourage everyone from doing ministry or reaching out to others in need; however, in times of crisis, there is proper training available that helps you know what to say and do in a given situation. In other words, if people have just watched several of their friends gunned down at school, it is not time to throw Bible tracts in their face and ask them if they know Jesus. Yes, I have personally seen these things happen and they are appalling at best. We must use common sense and think about how you would want to be treated in a similar situation.

In fact, the best Scripture to explain this process comes from the writings of Paul in the book of 2 Corinthians:

2 Corinthians 1:3–6

Blessed be the God and Father of our Lord Jesus Christ, the Father of mercies and God of all comfort, who comforts us in all our affliction, so that we may be able to comfort those who are in any affliction, with the comfort with which we ourselves are comforted by God. For as we share abundantly in Christ's sufferings, so through Christ we share abundantly in comfort too. If we are afflicted, it is for your comfort and salvation; and if we are comforted, it is for your comfort, which you experience when you patiently endure the same sufferings that we suffer.

EXAMPLE 3

This member has attended the church long enough to know everything about everybody. They can tell you about the new members, who they have only just met; they can tell you about the old members, who

71

they have talked about for years; and they can even tell you about the pastor and his wife. In fact, they know so much and are so superior in their spiritual life and intelligence that they can even tell the leadership how to run the church.

The Bible had a character like this named Jezebel, a heartless woman who would do anything to get her own way. Jezebel's actions created spiritual and moral disintegration in the kingdom and completely undermined the worship of Jehovah. She was such a negative factor in life that her name has come to stand for worldly wickedness of the worst type.

In the church, this Jezebel spirit is a prevalent one. It is subversive to the pastor, the ministry of God, and to the overall loving nature of the church body. Even those who try to stay away from Jezebel's influence are affected by the results of her seductive and disruptive power.

I want to remind you that Pastors spend their week praying for God's direction (at least they should be). Therefore, if they have sought God and have even been hired by the church body to do a job, isn't it in our best interest as a whole to follow their leadership?

It is also a fact that Pastors have a responsibility to God in shepherding the flock. This is a responsibility that I know pastors do not take lightly. From my personal experience as a pastor, I can tell you that this weighs very heavy on my heart. As I speak at churches and minister to others, I continually evaluate the things that I say and do. Are they pleasing to God? Did I say or do the right thing? Did my words today misdirect someone who heard them?

Furthermore, if I do feel that something is not right, I seek out wise counsel, I pray about the situations that I have encountered, and if need be, I go and apologize to the one who I believe I may have offended. However, when I walk according to God's Word and speak His truth, I do not worry about the outcome of what has occurred. I simply trust God to work in the life that I encountered and ask Him to bring conviction and help others to do what He has called them to do.

Remember, the pastor's job is to speak the Word of God and equip the saints to do God's work. It is also a part of a pastor's responsibility to keep peace among the believers. If you have ever studied the work of a shepherd, you will see that they sometimes take drastic measures to keep their sheep in line, and since the shepherd or pastor responsible for the church is dealing with issues that could be eternally condemning, don't you think it is important for him to deal with things that can be disruptive to the function of the church body?

While I am on the subject of the pastor, let me share this thought. When Jesus came to this earth, He came as a "servant leader." This is the same responsibility He has given to the pastors and ministers of the gospel. Unfortunately, I have watched through the years as this position has morphed into something very different than it was originally intended to be.

Today, many of our pastors have become "slave leaders." Yes, that is typed correctly—slave. In many churches, today the pastor is expected to teach everyone, discipline everyone, handle all the planning and business of the church, oversee the finances, plan and coordinate all evangelistic responsibilities in the community, and a plethora of additional duties. Oh yes, he is also responsible to preach, lead worship, and clean up the bathrooms at the end of the day. Since when did the servant become the slave?

Let me define my thoughts and use of the titles servant and slave. A servant is one who takes care of the master's business out of a sense of responsibility and love. Even in Bible times and the dark days of slavery around the world, there were those servants who admired and respected their masters. Sometimes they continued to serve their master long after their debt had been paid. Why? It was a labor of love. This is how Jesus came to earth. It was a labor of love designed by God the Father out of His love for us—and completed by Jesus out of His love for the Father.

Contrast that definition to that of a slave. A slave responds out of fear knows that if they do not do things correctly, or if they do not move fast enough to appease the owner, then they will be disciplined. It is their fear that drives their obedience and shapes their lives, a fear that also develops a disdain for the ones who unfairly push them so hard.

Look at it this way. Is your pastor a servant leader, one who comes to work each day excited about how he/she can be of service to the people? Do they look upon a loving crowd from the pulpit, knowing that whatever comes along, the people will support and uplift them in prayer and in work?

Or is your pastor a slave leader, one who responds out of fear of reprisal, looking out over the congregation on Sunday wondering who is going to attack him/her next? Which one of the angry sheep will pummel them today? What call will they get tonight while they are resting telling them everything they are doing wrong? Is this a pastor who is confident in his position and able to move freely at God's call, or is he threatened daily by the concern that he will lose his job and his family's income because he made the wrong person mad in church today?

If your pastor is the latter of these two examples, then the people of the church have become a hindrance and are limiting the effective ministry of the shepherd, something that God will not be pleased with along the way. Paul reminds us of that accountability in Hebrews 13:

Hebrews 13:15–17

Through him then let us continually offer up a sacrifice of praise to God, that is, the fruit of lips that acknowledge his name. Do not neglect to do good and to share what you have, for such sacrifices are pleasing to God. Obey your leaders and submit to them, for they are keeping watch over your souls, as those who will have to give an account. Let them do this with joy and not with groaning, for that would be of no advantage to you.

Once again, I am not trying to discourage. I am just trying to show that all of these issues are a part of the plan the enemy has put together to destroy the church, our families, and our spiritual lives. When he is able to destroy relationships, he begins to destroy everything important to our lives. Why? We are relational beings. We were made to rely on each other to survive and thrive in this world. We need each other to develop our strengths and encourage us through our weakness. The fact remains that we are stronger together than on our own.

One last issue I will address: church music. Every generation has their own beat. Some like a classical sound and others thrive on opera. Today, we hear hymns and contemporary Christian music. So what is best?

Maybe we should look at it in a different way. What reaches the majority of the people? What does God think about the whole thing? I think those are better questions. But wait—what does this have to do with friendly fire? The answer: go to any music pastor or music leader in the church and ask them to name some of the major conflicts in the church. It won't be long until that list includes music. It's too loud, it's too soft, it's not the right kind of music, the voices don't sound right, I can't sing with that worship leader—blah, blah, blah.

WE ARE STRONGER TOGETHER THAN ON OUR OWN.

Church, the music is not about how you feel. It is about worshiping God and giving praise to His name. Music is a way to lift up the name of Jesus and draw people into a place of worship on a corporate level. In reality, music has to reach the ears of the entire congregation and move them towards God together. This does not happen by music choice, but by the choice of the people to come into church with an attitude of worship and praise, an attitude that has been developed long before the church service starts by pursuing God during the week, on the way to service, and as we enter the doors.

Do I like all of the music I hear? No! However, if I have prayed prior to coming to church and arrived with an attitude to give instead of an attitude to take; then I have come for the right reason. Church is not a place for me to go to a show and be entertained. It is a place for me to love others, develop relationships, minister to my brothers and sisters, mentor others into a greater relationship with God, and be taught by the Shepherd of the flock. It is a place for me to enter into the very presence of God through corporate worship, a place for me to bring my heart of revival so that others may know Him in a better way.

Church services were never intended to be just my way and my house. It is God's house, and if He leads a music minister to share a certain song, then we should rejoice with them and watch how it brings others to Christ. If I don't like it, then I can stand there with hands lifted high giving praise and adoration to God for what He is going to do in the service that day.

Do you see? All of these are things that the enemy uses to disrupt and distract us from a full life with God. They are ways that he can destroy relationships, break up churches, and make us look like a laughing stock to the rest of the world.

Overall, the main goal of the enemy is to destroy life, and he does not care what tool he uses to complete that task. If he can destroy others by using us as one of his weapons, then he is more than happy to live with that result. By taking our misdirected words and unbridled actions, he can inflict wounds that disable and destroy lives; mentally, emotionally, financially, physically, and spiritually. Wounds that not only affect that individual, but also effect the relationship between the parties (allies) involved in the skirmish. Additionally, the devil knows that once these wounds are opened by friendly fire, they may be even more difficult to repair than those inflicted by the enemy himself.

In all of this friendly fire, there is an additional factor to consider. As a warrior is wounded, their effectiveness in the spiritual battle is diminished. One who was previously seen as a strong and mighty warrior for God can be reduced to a whimpering and fearful man. Through years of constant battle and the effect of personal betrayal, the trust and faith that the warrior once carried is crushed. In this case, the things they believed in previously are questioned, and the very soul of the fighter can be at risk.

To combat these detrimental effects, we must understand the weapons that we wield for God. We must discipline ourselves to learn how to implement them properly and understand the ramifications that exist if we fail in the effort. At the same time, we must follow the orders of God, as He works in and though us to unleash the power that lies in the palm of His hand. We must faithfully use His weapons, power, and authority to defend our position, ultimately obtaining for us an overwhelming victory. In short, we must use these spiritual assets effectively for us to succeed in the things of God. Otherwise, our continued miscommunication, incompetence, disobedience, and dissension will cause us to fail in the completion of our mission. This failure would have catastrophic and eternal results.

Think about this: in the Old Testament, when the people of God began to follow their own ways and acted in with selfish motives, they were disciplined in very harsh ways.

To those who disobeyed God and lacked faith to enter the Promised Land:

Numbers 14:20–23

Then the Lord said, "I have pardoned, according to your word. But truly, as I live, and as all the earth shall be filled with the glory of the Lord, none of the men who have seen my glory and my signs that I did in Egypt and in the wilderness, and yet have put me to the test these ten times and have not obeyed my voice, shall see the land that I swore to give to their fathers. And none of those who despised me shall see it..."

When the people of God disobeyed the commands of Moses as directed by God and rebelled:

And Moses said, "Hereby you shall know that the Lord has sent me to do all these works, and that it has not been of my own accord. If these men die as all men die, or if they are visited by the fate of all mankind, then the Lord has not sent me. But if the Lord creates something new, and the ground opens its mouth and swallows them up with all that belongs to them, and they go down alive into Sheol, then you shall know that these men have despised the Lord." And as soon as he had finished speaking all these words, the ground under them split apart. And the earth opened its mouth and swallowed them up, with their households and all the people who belonged to Korah and all their goods. So they and all that belonged to them went down alive into Sheol, and the earth closed over them, and they perished from the midst of the assembly.

As I have shared stories like this in the past with different people, they are quick to remind me that this was under a God of wrath; now we live under grace, and God no longer disciplines people in this way. When I hear that I get very concerned. First, we are negating the fact that we are commanded to follow the decrees of God and are directed to live out our lives as Jesus did, by serving God. In addition to these biblical facts, we must also understand that continual disobedience to the things of God limits the effectiveness of ministry on the earth, thereby negating the things that God may be able to do in a given church or individual. This disruption of the process of God to reach all people is a direct violation of His purpose in sending Jesus to the earth to restore the lost. That, in and of itself, is not a place where I would lay my head very often.

CONTINUAL DISOBEDIENCE TO THE THINGS OF GOD LIMITS THE EFFECTIVENESS OF MINISTRY ON THE EARTH.

When we disobey God continually, our heart is deceitful, or we regularly undermine the work that God wants to accomplish, there may come a time when He is just fed up with our garbage. Here is one last story to remember about disobedience and God's discipline from the New Testament.

But a man named Ananias, with his wife Sapphira, sold a piece of property, and with his wife's knowledge he kept back for himself some of the proceeds and brought only a part of it and laid it at the apostles' feet. But Peter said, "Ananias, why has Satan filled your heart to lie to the Holy Spirit and to keep back for yourself part of the proceeds of the land? While it remained unsold, did it not remain your own? And after it was sold, was it not at your disposal? Why is it that you have contrived this deed in your heart? You have not lied to man but to God." When Ananias heard these words, he fell down and breathed his last. And great fear came upon all who heard of it. The young men rose and wrapped him up and carried him out and buried him. After an interval of about three hours his wife came in, not knowing what had happened. And Peter said to her, "Tell me whether you sold the land for so much." And she said, "Yes, for so much." But Peter said to her, "How is it that you have agreed together to test the Spirit of the Lord? Behold, the feet of those who have buried your husband are at the door, and they will carry you out." Immediately she fell down at his feet and breathed her last. When the young men came in they found her dead, and they carried her out and buried her beside her husband. And great fear came upon the whole church and upon all who heard of these things.

Church, Jesus is coming soon. He needs warriors, not spies. There is enough evil in the world for us to fight, so why don't we work together and stop our friendly fire destruction of those who we are commanded to love. This is something that we have all been guilty of at some point in life. So today with me, ask God to forgive you and move on before it is too late for us and for the dying world that surrounds us each day.

Keep this thought in the back of your mind: Many people die because God is just done watching them destroy the church and the people around them. Don't make Him tired of you.

1 Corinthians 11:30–32

That is why many of you are weak and ill, and some have died. But if we judged ourselves truly, we would not be judged. But when we are judged by the Lord, we are disciplined so that we may not be condemned along with the world.

In your church experience, have you ever seen or experienced these destructive friendly fire issues in your own life? Do you ever wonder why so many people have left the churches you have been a part of through the years? Have you been on the receiving end of some of this nonsense? It is one of the reasons there are so many denominations and church plants. People through the ages have been so disgusted by those around them that they leave and start something else. Unfortunately, I have learned that people are people no matter where you go. Therefore, if you leave a church due to these kinds of problems, you will eventually run into someone else like them again in the next church, or you will carry your own hurt and attitude to another group and become a part of the problem, creating your own friendly fire.

BATTLE PLAN

WE MUST

1. Become an encourager. Tell those around us how important they are in our lives. Express our love to each other every time we attend church.

2. Forgive those who have offended us. We may recall the Scripture that says: if we cannot forgive others, God cannot forgive us. We need God's forgiveness daily.

3. Encourage and pray for our pastors and their spouses. Each of us will benefit from becoming a part of the team, and the encouragement will free the pastor to complete the tasks that God has called him to accomplish in our churches.

4. Encourage and support other church staff. If God has called them to be a part of our ministry team, it is our responsibility to be a part of their success.

5. Always be in prayer, preparing ourselves to enter into corporate praise and worship. Setting aside our own plans and seeking only the plans of God as we gather together. Who does He want to reach? What lives will be changed as we become a spiritual force in this world of darkness?

DEVOTIONAL

This was a very difficult chapter to write, and I thought many times that I should take it out of the book. However, it is one of the issues that has done the most damage to the church as a whole and to our witness to the unsaved world. Therefore, I chose to tackle a subject that the Bible exposes, but very few people have discussed. Hopefully, my effort will do more good than harm?

In what way has "friendly fire" (the negative actions or words of other believers) negatively affected my life?

_____

_____

_____

_____

_____

_____

_____

In what ways has "friendly fire" in the Christian world impacted my friends, my family, and my church?

_____

_____

_____

_____

_____

_____

_____

How does the non-believer view this "friendly fire" in the church world?

_____

_____

_____

_____

_____

_____

How have I been a part of this negative attitude in the past?

_____

_____

_____

_____

_____

_____

What can I do to encourage good behavior and hold my fellow believers accountable for their words and actions? (Proverbs 27:17, Galatians 6:1-2, Matthew 18:15-17, James 5:16)

_____

_____

_____

_____

_____

_____

How can I hold myself accountable for my words and actions? (Matthew 12:36–37, Romans 14:12)

_____

_____

_____

_____

_____

_____

How can I listen more closely to God and be obedient to Him?

_____

_____

_____

_____

_____

_____

What steps can I take to encourage others and become a more positive Christian role model?

_____

_____

_____

_____

_____

Note: Each of us have done wrong in the church and against other Christians. Therefore, instead of throwing stones at the ones we feel are guilty, remember that as it pertains to this subject we all live in glass houses, so be careful about throwing rocks. You may cause your own house to crumble.

PRAYER:

Lord, help me to forgive those who have wronged me. Whether it was an actual offense, or just one that I have perceived. God take away any anger or resentment that I may have towards them and allow me to accept them fully as Your child and my co-laborer for Your Kingdom. I ask Lord, that You also forgive me for the things that I have done against others and that anyone who was offended by me would find grace in their heart on my behalf. Father, if there is someone I need to apologize to, arrange it in Your perfect time and give me the words to say that will bring healing and restoration to our relationship. Lord, also help me to support my pastor and his/her family. Remind me to pray for them daily, for the leadership of our church and for our congregation. Thank you Lord for loving me, even when I fall.

THE ATTACK ON THE FAMILY

7

As I stated earlier, our enemy is a terrorist. He uses hit and run tactics against the weak and defenseless. One of the greatest weapons he uses is the destruction of the family. Just like his attacks on our relationship with God, the devil knows that when he can destroy the family relationship he undermines the very core of our society. He knows that if he can destroy our relationships on this earth, then he can redirect our thoughts and our emotions. This is accomplished as he directs us to pursue our problems and focus on the pain caused by unfulfilled dreams. By taking our focus off of God, he can then destroy everything around us.

Evil began this family battle by causing discourse between brothers. Look again at a story from Genesis 4, we see the sons of Adam, one a shepherd and one a farmer. As the story goes, Abel (the shepherd) brought a better sacrifice to God by giving the firstborn of his flock as an offering. This act of obedience and sacrificial giving pleased God and He honored Abel with His favor. This angered Cain (the farmer), and he allowed thoughts of sin to seize him. God warned Cain that sin was crouched at his door and that he needed to do what was right to overcome it, but in disobedience to God, he lured Abel into a field and killed him.

This conflict sounds so much like many in the church today—people within the same body of Christ jockeying for position. Each one working so hard to have their own way, that they become a tool of the devil in destroying the unity of the church body. I have seen this first hand, and it is a gruesome thing to watch.

It occurs when a few people in the church begin to think that their agenda is more important than the body as a whole. Through selfish thoughts and motives, they begin to undermine everything that leadership has put into place even to the point that they disregard the divine direction God has given for the church.

I am not just talking about church elections, boards, or members. I am talking about Christians in general, who continually place their own wants over the things of God. Remember, these are not lost sinners who have never attended church; they are the people who have taught classes in a Sunday school. They are the ones who at one time we looked up to and followed every word that proceeded from their mouth. Now, all of a sudden, they have become a wolf in sheep's clothing seeking only to devour anyone who gets too close to their jaws of hate and discontent.

Let me make a point by using the words that define these kinds of people in the church. They are unhappy, spread discontent wherever they go, and usually have something bad to say about the pastor and his leadership team. They try to undermine everything positive in the church and usually have no interest in reaching their community for Christ. They come to dinners hoping to see a failure they can expose and attend services to find things they disagree with from the pulpit. They gossip in the bathroom, tell lies in the hallways, and then raise their hands in the sanctuary to give praise to God. In short, these fellow believers are no more than dissension driving examples of heretics. They are the religious Pharisees of our day. What they say with their mouth and teach through their actions is nothing more than a falsehood of God's truth. One day, their undermining ways are going to place them in the presence of a God who will ask, "Why?"

"Why did you work to destroy the family that I was so desperately trying to build?"

"Why did you think that your personal agenda and emotions were more important than the lost souls that I was trying to reach by the direction of my Holy Spirit?"

"Who do you think you are that your own ways are higher than the ways of the living God?"

"Did you not hear me when I said, 'love one another?'" (John 13:34)

"And what part of My Word that says 'gossip is a sin' did you not understand?" (Romans 1:28–32)

Friends, I believe that there are going to be consequences for those who have caused these "little ones" to walk away. Young believers who came into your church and were so distressed by the things they saw people doing that they ran as far from God as they could.

What other family conflicts do we see in the church? How about the unforgiveness that exists between people in the same congregation? The Bible clearly instructs us to forgive. God is vehemently opposed to an unforgiving attitude. He even declares in Scripture that if we are unforgiving of others, we will remain unforgiven by Him.

Matthew 6:14–15

For if you forgive others their trespasses, your heavenly Father will also forgive you, but if you do not forgive others their trespasses, neither will your Father forgive your trespasses.

Is that what we want? Are some of us so bent on our hatred of others that we are willing to sacrifice our soul for our own selfishness? You see, that is what unforgiveness is all about—selfishness. The reason I do not want to forgive someone is because I want vengeance; I want them to suffer for what they did to me—or perhaps more realistically, what I think they did to me.

UNFORGIVENESS IS ALL ABOUT SELFISHNESS.

I have found in many cases that the facts that surround an unforgiving heart are not facts at all; they are merely perceptions made by a confused and weak-minded person, a person who cannot see far enough beyond their own pain to embrace the kindness of another.

Now, you may think that this is not a viable subject for this book. You may also believe that these kinds of things do not exist in the church. Let me take a moment to verify my rant on these destructive behaviors by sharing a quote from a "loving" Christian person in a church where I was the senior pastor. This was a person who made great claims about all they had done for God, one who gloriously proclaimed their own stories of sacrificial service to that church body for many years, a person who cried real tears when biblically confronted about the problems that they caused with others and defended themselves in private and in public by throwing out accusations against other believers. This is the person that my wife and I personally heard say, "I will never forgive that person and will never work with them again in this church."

I think you get the point. We love them anyway and feel sorry for them. In fact, I will say at this point that all of the things that have been done against us, we have forgiven. Even though I have made these statements, I do not hold grudges towards anyone. In reality, we actually feel a spiritual pity for those who have acted out against us and recognize that God would help them get past all of this pain if they would let Him.

From the other people's point of view, we have probably offended people in different ways at different times, for that we are sorry, and many times we have said that to their face and from the pulpit in a public setting. When we did offend, it was never a malicious act, and we never intended to hurt anyone. Whether that hurt is real or perceived, it still hurt to that person, and we apologize for that. To any who have offended us in any way, whether real or perceived, we also forgive you and trust God to take you to new heights by His never-ending grace and abundant love. We pray blessing upon you and ask God to open the floodgates of heaven upon your life so that you can prosper in every way.

Folks, as I have pointed out, the devil works very hard to destroy the relationships that we have with other people, and this is what I have tried to express in these previous paragraphs. However, this destruction is not confined to the church. The devil works constantly to create dissension at work and in the home. He uses the jealousy of success and the fear of racial inequality to fire up the people of the world. This destruction of relationship peaks as it expands into confrontation between nations, thereby triggering war and acts of terrorism that are so prevalent in our world today. Although road rage may be a new concept in our society, confrontation and the destruction of relationships is not. The reality is that all people of the world are adversely affected by this tactic of relational destruction.

How many times have we looked at a Christian friend or church member and been upset because they have experienced great success? We begin to have thoughts of greed and envy wondering why we can't be blessed in such a way. Why does it seem that they are always getting "the good stuff," and I am always getting the garbage?

This attitude in itself goes against the personality of a true Christian. We are to be helpful to others and always hoping that they do well, especially to those who are of the household of Christ.

In the New Testament, Paul dealt sternly with the battles taking place in the church. In 1 Corinthians, he speaks of the quarreling that has taken place between brothers.

1 Corinthians 1:10–19

I appeal to you, brothers, by the name of our Lord Jesus Christ, that all of you agree, and that there be no divisions among you, but that you be united in the same mind and the same judgment. For it has been reported to me by Chloe's people that there is quarreling among you, my brothers. What I mean is that each one of you says, "I follow Paul," or "I follow Apollos," or "I follow Cephas," or "I follow Christ." Is Christ divided? Was Paul crucified for you? Or were you baptized in the name of Paul? I thank God that I baptized none of you except Crispus and Gaius, so that no one may say that you were baptized in my name.(I did baptize also the household of Stephanas. Beyond that, I do not know whether I baptized anyone else.) For Christ did not send me to baptize but to preach the gospel, and not with words of eloquent wisdom, lest the cross of Christ be emptied of its power. For the word of the cross is folly to those who are perishing, but to us who are being saved it is the power of God. For it is written, "I will destroy the wisdom of the wise, and the discernment of the discerning I will thwart."

You see the devil is a cunning adversary that can take one small issue and turn it into nuclear destruction just by pressing a few of the right buttons. It is the small things in life that can become overwhelming difficulties if we fail to recognize that spiritual warfare is the source of our many problems. In the church especially, we must be aware of the destructive force that comes against us. By invading the thoughts and actions of the people of God, the enemy can undermine our testimony. This causes the world to see us for who we are and hides from them the real message of God's love, mercy, and grace. That is what makes church dissension one of the biggest factors in our failed efforts to share the gospel with the lost. Why would a hurting world want to escape from sin just to be a part of another dysfunctional family?

What kind of positive difference can we make if we work to maintain the attitude of a servant who seeks only to please our master by placing the benefit of others ahead of our own? If we can learn to make this one of our highest goals, we will work hard to please others, and in doing so, we will become more pleasing to God. In fact, it is this attitude of love and sacrifice that will cause the world to see something that they will not be able to explain in earthly terms. They will recognize the love of Christ in us, and it will afford us opportunities to share His ways with them.

John 13:34–35

A new commandment I give to you, that you love one another: just as I have loved you, you also are to love one another. By this all people will know that you are my disciples, if you have love for one another.

This change in attitude would make a positive difference in our churches, increase our joy in life, and become a catalyst for revival in our world.

As we have traveled and ministered across the country, we have seen too much of this from church to church. Organizations that have begun to believe so strongly in their banner, that they have forgotten the overall purpose of the kingdom mindset. God is not about denomination or affiliation. God is all about recovering lost souls and bringing them into His kingdom. His purpose lies in the facts surrounding His own words—"that none should perish."

When will we get on board with that thought and seek only to reach others for Christ? When will we take on the servant leader role as Jesus taught and place our own agenda behind the agenda of God?

GOD IS ALL ABOUT RECOVERING LOST SOULS AND BRINGING THEM INTO HIS KINGDOM.

Instead, within our families today, we become embittered toward one another. Instead of taking on the face of God, we have accepted the face of the world, and like with the rest of the world, our dysfunction continues. If we are to become warriors of God, we must hear

God's warning. We must stop the internal conflict within our families and our churches so that we can spread the joy and love of Christ to the world. We must develop proper attitudes and obedience to God so that we can create proper lifestyles. It is then, and only then, that our churches' divorce rates will decline; it is only then that church splits will become a minor statistic; and it is only then that we will see our children, our friends, and our neighbors come back to a loving relationship with Jesus Christ.

Do you want to see a revival? Then let God start one in your heart. Become one of the catalysts to the move of God in your generation. Stop being a bystander, and become one who stands by God in all things. Be a warrior, and stand up for what is right, no matter who comes against you.

BATTLE PLAN

WE MUST

1. Seek only to please God. The questions we should ask ourselves each day is these: Am I pleasing God? Are my words and actions conveying an attitude of true Christian service as one who belongs to Jesus Christ?

2. Strive towards a conscious effort to be used by God in every situation. Today, are we peacemakers or workers? Our roles in God's army change by the minute, and like Paul, we should seek to be all things to all people so that they may know Christ.

3. Seek revival in our own hearts. Too many people think that revival comes from praying for a revival or having an evangelist come and speak. The reality is that revival comes through the heart of the individuals. True revival in a church or a city starts with individual revival and spreads to those we come in contact with in our lives. Think of revival as a good virus. Once I get infected with it and live out its joy, it will automatically infect those around me.

What kind of positive difference can I make by becoming a servant of Christ to others?

_____

_____

_____

_____

_____

_____

What can I do to be sure my actions and words please God?

_____

_____

_____

_____

_____

How can I place the needs of others ahead of my own personal needs?

_____

_____

_____

_____

_____

Remember: The very Son of God (God Himself) set aside His position and authority in heaven to serve His Father. He also became a servant leader to those around Him. Although He was greater than everyone, He humbled Himself "even unto death on the cross" so that others may be saved. How much more should we humble ourselves to serve Him?

PRAYER:

Lord, grant me an overwhelming attitude of love. Give me a sacrificial heart so that I may be willing to serve You in any capacity on this earth. Lord, help me to be all things to all people so that they may be saved, and light a fire of revival in the very depths of my heart. May You be greatly blessed and honored by all that I say and do in the name of Jesus. Amen.

THE BATTLE FOR MARRIAGE

8

E vil also seeks to destroy the relationship in a marriage. When this takes place, many lives are torn apart. The couple, extended families, and their friends are all affected by the separation of the pair. If there are children involved, then that destruction is extended even further. It not only effects their current situation, but also becomes a mental and emotional scar that can compound the destruction of relationships for generations to come.

Many statistics can be viewed that show how the destruction of a marriage and the resulting family break up can affect our society. Studies have shown that a large number of sociopathic criminals were adversely affected by the twisted relationships that they have experienced in the past, experiences that placed them in a family setting that undermined their mental and emotional structure. These studies also show that many criminals are the result of dysfunctional homes, where they were ignored or abused, instead of loved and appreciated. This process not only affects how they think, but can also corrupt the overall condition of their life. When left untreated, this instability causes them to lash out at everything around them. The resulting sin and destruction flows into every aspect of their lives as they become a nemesis to their circle of influence.

During my work on the streets as a United States Marshal, my path crossed the lives of these people many times. These men and women alike had been completely rejected as children by their own families because they were brought into families through sinful relationships. Young boys and girls had witnessed abusive behavior by a father or mother because the marriage vows were either ignored or a proper marriage did not exist.

The streets of America and the world are full of these dysfunctional families that base their relationships on the things of the world and the evil desires of their own hearts. In my personal experience, I have encountered children who were directed by their own parents to sell drugs on the street for the family business. I have seen girls and boys forced into prostitution in order to make money for their mother or father. I have talked to children who have been sexually abused by parents, grandparents, momma's latest boyfriend, or some neighbor down the street.

IF WE ARE GOING TO BE WARRIORS, WE HAVE TO STAND AGAINST THE THINGS THAT UNDERMINE THE WORK OF GOD.

These are people that have been treated as property or livestock. They were never loved unconditionally or accepted for who they are. They have never witnessed a proper marriage that shows unconditional love. They have never experienced the sacrifice of a husband that only wants his wife to accomplish her own dreams. Their view of life together in a family is a facade of pleasing others so that they can be accepted. Unfortunately, their lack of knowledge in this area of life causes them to become another statistic in our society. Their lives are being played out for the wrong crowd, a crowd of uneducated, uncaring, and lawless creatures that dwell in the underbelly of our society. In this crowd, their only goal is self-satisfaction at the cost of everyone around them. They are people who show no love or mercy, but rule those around them through fear and manipulation. They are full of lies and bear nothing but bad fruit.

Matthew 12:33–35

Either make the tree good and its fruit good, or make the tree bad and its fruit bad, for the tree is known by its fruit. You brood of vipers! How can you speak good, when you are evil? For out of the abundance of the heart the mouth speaks. The good person out of his good treasure brings forth good, and the evil person out of his evil treasure brings forth evil.

This takes us to another scripture dealing with improper relationships, one that has become a destruction of the marriage covenant in our world today. Hang on, reader; this one will also bring great tribulation to those who stand for what is right according to God's Word.

Romans 1:20–32

For his invisible attributes, namely, his eternal power and divine nature, have been clearly perceived, ever since the creation of the world, in the things that have been made. So they are without excuse. For although they knew God, they did not honor him as God or give thanks to him, but they became futile in their thinking, and their foolish hearts were darkened. Claiming to be wise, they became fools, and exchanged the glory of the immortal God for images resembling mortal man and birds and animals and creeping things. Therefore God gave them up in the lusts of their hearts to impurity, to the dishonoring of their bodies among themselves, because they exchanged the truth about God for a lie and worshiped and served the creature rather than the Creator, who is blessed forever! Amen. For this reason God gave them up to dishonorable passions. For their women exchanged natural relations for those that are contrary to nature; and the men likewise gave up natural relations with women and were consumed with passion for one another, men committing shameless acts with men and receiving in themselves the due penalty for their error. And since they did not see fit to acknowledge God, God gave them up to a debased mind to do what ought not to be done. They were filled with all manner of unrighteousness, evil, covetousness, malice. They are full of envy, murder, strife, deceit, maliciousness. They are gossips, slanderers, haters of God, insolent, haughty, boastful, inventors of evil, disobedient to parents, foolish, faithless, heartless, ruthless. Though they know God's righteous decree that those who practice such things deserve to die, they not only do them but give approval to those who practice them.

If we are going to be warriors, we have to stand against the things that undermine the work of God. That means that we must take on sin. We must call it what it is and not back down from the sufferings our stand may subject us to. If we are going to deal with marriage and relationships, then we must deal with it from a proper biblical perspective.

If we look at the scripture above, it does not just mention homosexual acts, but it also mentions sexual perversion in general. If you look closely, it goes on to say that those who agree with these acts or approve them in any way are in possession of the same kind of depraved minds as those who commit the acts.

What does that mean? It means that if there is an individual, pastor, politician, church, organization, or government that approves of this evil, then they themselves are just as guilty as those who commit the evil before God. This is not my condemnation of their attitudes and actions. This is the condemnation of God Himself.

In our world today, the devil has used every kind of perversion he can use to undermine marriage and the family. In fact, it has become such an issue that now pastors, churches, and wedding cake bakers have been sued in court for not participating in these immoral acts by performing their services for those involved in the sin.

Imagine that. Our world has sunk to such a low state that it is difficult for a righteous person to stand in his own beliefs. Now if you don't see that as spiritual warfare, you might as well cover our eyes and wait for hell to freeze over. This is not only sin and spiritual warfare, but it is a direct attack on the people of God and the Word of God itself.

This is why we need spiritual warriors to stand in the gap for our nation and for our world. We need men and women who will rise up to fight this battle through prayer and fasting, warriors who will take on legislative rights and begin to stand against this onslaught of the enemy. If we don't stand, if warriors do not rise up, then our children have no hope, and the world they face will be even fuller of evil than what we see today.

Virtually every TV show you see today has to have some example of a broken marriage, a very sexually active man or woman, or a homosexual relationship. Many commercials promote gay couples kissing or have some type of gay connotation. Frankly, I am getting sick of having this concept forced into my everyday life. I can hardly walk down the street without seeing two girls hugging each other or two guys kissing.

Yes, I realize all of this sin is out there and that it has been practiced on the earth since soon after the fall of mankind. If it were not a problem in the days of the Bible, then it would not have been dealt with in Scripture, so it is true that there is nothing new under the sun. However, this does not mean that I have to watch it and live with it every day.

In this case, Scripture is clear that we are to love the sinner. From that point of view, I do care about all people and pray that one day everyone would come to know Jesus in a new way. However, I was never directed by God to love the sin. Therefore, it is the sin that I stand against and not the person who commits it.

Now to those who believe differently than I have stated about this subject specifically, I pray for you and trust that God will find a way to show you how much you are loved for who He made you to be, and not what your situation or society has told you that you are. You are a child of God, created to do His will. If you were born a male, then He did not make a mistake, and it is a man you should be. If you were born female, then you are beautiful the way He made you, and there is no reason to change that position. Love God, live for God, and seek out the desires of your heart by trusting Him for all things, as you follow the Scriptures He has placed before us.

BATTLE PLAN

WE MUST

1. Treat our spouses as directed by scripture. Men, we are to love our wives as God loved the church. That means that we would give our very life, so that she may have abundance in every part of the marriage relationship. Love, nurture, provide, protect, etc. It also includes proper communication. We are **not** kings over subservient wives; we are spiritual leaders of the household that gain respect by leading in a proper biblical way, being examples of godliness in our relationships. Men, why do we act so thoughtless sometimes, even to the point of destroying the one who God says is "bone of my bone and flesh of my flesh?"

2. Respect and support our husbands. Ladies, why do we nitpick and complain to our friends, family, and spouse over every little issue. What happened to grace, compassion, and understanding? Where are the Proverbs 31 women of our generation? Do we not understand that all the while a man is trying to do his best, he is being pummeled every day by a world that wants to see him fail? The part of the wife is to encourage, uplift, support, and motivate her man, according to God's plan.

3. Be sure, as parents, that our marriage relationship is a positive example to our children and our extended families. Do not undermine it by talking bad about each other to our children, family, and friends. As Scripture states, if we have a problem with that person, we go to that person and discuss it like adults. Yes, this applies to our spouses. We need to stop the gossip in our own relationship and work together so that we can both succeed. There has been enough divorce, and God hates divorce!

Note: Much of this issue is made worse by the fact that so many marriages have failed. Few people today have been given the opportunity to see a proper biblical marriage, a true covenant relationship. If you know of one, then seek counsel from those who are succeeding. If you are one seek, opportunities to help those who struggle. Whichever scenario you find yourself in, do something to change the disasters that are taking place in our churches today. It is this issue of poor marriage relationships that is helping to unravel the very fabric of our society.

Begin today to seek God in a new way. Ask Him to guide us in our marriage and family relationships. Study the biblical principles of a proper marriage and become the catalyst for a new fire in our own life. Remember, we loved that person enough to become a part of his or her life forever. This was a promise made before God Himself. Now we must do everything we can to keep that promise. Too many lives are depending on it!

This is a battle that not everyone on Earth will fight. However, it is a battle that will in some way affect everyone on Earth. Evil knows that if the relationship in our marriages can be destroyed, then the magnitude of the destruction can be multiplied. In that destruction, the married couple, their children, extended families, friends, and even society are all affected by the separation of the pair, an effect that can go on for generations, as new and destructive attitudes are developed in the aftermath. These are the mental and emotional scars that can take decades to overcome and, many times, can only be resolved by the work of God.

What steps can I take to become a better spouse? (Ephesians 5:22–33)

_____

_____

_____

_____

_____

_____

_____

What can I do to be a better parent? (Proverbs 22:6, Proverbs 23:13–14)

_____

_____

_____

_____

_____

_____

What positive actions and statements can I direct towards my spouse in public that will be a good Christian witness to others? (Colossians 3:12–14)

_____

_____

_____

_____

_____

What actions can I take to make sure I am at peace with my spouse and others who may be hurt by my words or actions? (Romans 12:18, Hebrews 12:14)

_____

_____

_____

_____

_____

How can I help children affected by divorce in a positive way? (Isaiah 30:20–21)

_____

_____

_____

_____

_____

Note: Divorce may have placed you in a very difficult position. Do the best you can, and look to God for wisdom and direction as you move forward in life. If you have been directly involved in a divorce, know that you are loved and God can forgive any and all sin. Do not allow the enemy to destroy you and those around you by placing unbearable guilt upon your life. If you have asked God's forgiveness for any wrong doing on your part, you have been redeemed. Walk in His peace and His presence.

9

LACK OF KNOWLEDGE AND NON-EXISTENCE OF GOD

Another weapon of the enemy is the thought of a non-existent devil. Many people who do not know Christ, and even some that do, have accepted the lie that the devil does not exist. Satan himself causes them to believe that evil spirits are just fairy tales developed for books and movies, or that these stories have been written to strike fear in man's mind to make them live a clean and sinless life. Those who believe this deception can live an ineffective Christian life or a life that denies sin altogether and ultimately leads them to eternal damnation.

These are the same people who do not want to accept the laws of God. This attitude of non-existence allows them to operate in their ruthless and disobedient ways without fear of reprisal. It becomes a shield for their soul, put in place by the enemy to limit their exposure to conviction. They follow a path of destruction with very little, if any, remorse for the acts they have committed. But one day, they will face judgment and their unbelief will be shattered.

Ephesians 5:1–7

Therefore be imitators of God, as beloved children. And walk in love, as Christ loved us and gave himself up for us, a fragrant offering and sacrifice to God. But sexual immorality and all impurity or covetousness must not even be named among you, as is proper among saints. Let there be no filthiness nor foolish talk nor crude joking, which are out of place, but instead let there be thanksgiving. For you may be sure of this, that everyone who is sexually immoral or impure, or who is covetous (that is, an idolater), has no inheritance in the kingdom of Christ and God. Let no one deceive you with empty words, for because of these things the wrath of God comes upon the sons of disobedience. Therefore do not become partners with them.

I have seen similar realizations of guilt take place during federal court cases. A cool and overly confident young thug will strut up to the judge's bench as his fate is declared. When the verdict of guilty is announced, he may just shrug and smile like he is the one who holds the world by the tail. But then, the judge speaks, and lays out the result of the guilty verdict and begins to discuss the levels of sentencing that are available to him. With this being a federal case, it is much different than what the offender may have dealt with before in county or state court. Then that sentence enters the ears of the 20-year-old, young man: "Ten years minimum mandatory for conspiracy, five years minimum mandatory for the guns and 30 years on each of the three felony charges. All adding up to a total of 105 years. Due to the severity of the crimes, each sentence will run consecutive to the others." You can imagine the fear and disbelief has he realizes that his actions have placed him in prison for the rest of his life without any chance of parole.

I have shared these stories about the criminals that I watched during my career with others. As they stood before that federal judge, they were surprised by the courts declarations and guidelines. They could not believe the extent of the power wielded in that setting and were further astonished at the length of the sentence pronounced upon them for their crimes. They would state that they did not know that could happen or that they could be held accountable at that level for the actions of their partners under the law as it pertains to a conspiracy. As the punishment was read, they contemplated the lost years, and you could see the realization, as it would hit them in a flood of emotion. Then, after stating the sentence, the judge would just look at them and proclaim, "I guess that is something you should have thought about before you committed the crime."

EACH OF US WILL BE HELD ACCOUNTABLE BY GOD FOR THE THINGS THAT WE DO AND THE THINGS THAT WE FAIL TO DO ACCORDING TO GOD'S WORD.

You see, we can claim ignorance of the law or we can claim that the penalty is unfair. We can say that we did not know or that we just did not believe what everyone told us. However, it will be irrelevant to the issue at hand when we stand before God on judgment day. At that time, He will be our final Judge and His sentence will be for eternity. No pardons available, no appeals, and no chance to change our minds at that time, just a short walk towards a long fall into hell. In this, the Bible is very clear. Each of us will be held accountable by God for the things that we do and the things that we fail to do according to God's Word (1 Corinthians 3:13–15). If we have rejected His Son Jesus Christ as Savior, then our fate will be sealed and our day of judgment will be final. For some, that will be an eternally fatal decision, no matter what excuse we attempt to employ.

That brings us to another issue related to non-existence. That is the non-existence of God, His Son Jesus, and the Holy Spirit. People deny any existence of God claiming that they do not believe in "those kind of things." Others have stated that they believe Jesus was just a good actor and fooled a lot of people. Still others claim that this idea of God is for those who are too weak to live life on their own. Unfortunately, if we choose to believe the lie that God does not exist, then we face a dreary future and an even worse eternity.

In fact, if we compare the claims of the non-believers to the facts of history (not just the Bible), you see that their claims are made in complete ignorance. Many books authored by many writers (who were not Christians) declare the existence of Jesus and miracles of God. Many of the scribes of Egypt who wrote down every detail of a Pharaoh's reign, tell in their history the same things declared in Jewish history and in the Bible.

For example, J. Warner Wallace in his book *Cold-Case Christianity*, mentions a report by Sextus Julius Africanus written around 221 AD. In this report, Africanus quotes a secular writer named Thallus who in 52 AD wrote an account of the scene at the cross and attempted to explain away the sudden darkness that had occurred that day.

Thallus (52 AD) was an early secular writer that mentioned Jesus. However, his writings no longer exist. But Africanus, writing around 221 AD quoted Thallus who previously tried to explain away the darkness occurring at Jesus' crucifixion:

> On the whole world there pressed a most fearful darkness; and the rocks were rent by an earthquake, and many places in Judea and other districts were thrown down. This darkness Thallus, in the third book of his History, calls, as appears to me without reason, an eclipse of the sun. (Sextus Julius Africanus, Chronography, 18:1) (See the book *Cold-Case Christianity* by J. Warner Wallace for more on this subject.)

Through the years even scientists have determined that the only way to verify certain things on earth is to compare them to biblical accounts. Geologists, archaeologists, and others have uncovered historical sites that reveal specific details of the Bible story that they reflect.

For example, the World News Daily Report on the possible discovery of the biblical cities Sodom and Gomorrah. The article entitled *Jordan: Archaeologists Could Have Uncovered Biblical City Of Sodom* tells us of a team of archaeologists lead by Professor Steven Collins, uncovering a site that seemed to be the ancient destroyed city of Sodom. The article goes on to tell us that the site seemed to be destroyed by some kind of volcanic disaster at approximately the same time that the Bible describes the event of the annihilations of Sodom and Gomorrah. (*You can read the whole article at http://worldnewsdailyreport.com/jordan-archaeologists-could-have-uncovered-biblical-city-of-sodom/*)

Why do some people spend so much time trying to disprove Scripture? Are they so set against God that they do not care what He thinks about their efforts to discredit Him?

But what does God say about His existence? Let's look at His words, since they are ultimately the only words that matter.

Psalm 19:1–5

The heavens declare the glory of God, and the sky above proclaims his handiwork. Day to day pours out speech, and night to night reveals knowledge. There is no speech, nor are there words, whose voice is not heard. Their voice goes out through all the earth, and their words to the end of the world. In them he has set a tent for the sun, which comes out like a bridegroom leaving his chamber, and, like a strong man, runs its course with joy.

Romans 1:18–20

For the wrath of God is revealed from heaven against all ungodliness and unrighteousness of men, who by their unrighteousness suppress the truth. For what can be known about God is plain to them, because God has shown it to them. For his invisible attributes, namely, his eternal power and divine nature, have been clearly perceived, ever since the creation of the world, in the things that have been made. So they are without excuse.

1 Corinthians 8:5–6

For although there may be so-called gods in heaven or on earth—as indeed there are many "gods" and many "lords"—yet for us there is one God, the

Father, from whom are all things and for whom we exist, and one Lord, Jesus Christ, through whom are all things and through whom we exist.

Therefore, if we believe that God does exist, then how do we go about finding Him? First, we must have a little faith.

Hebrews 11:6

And without faith it is impossible to please him, for whoever would draw near to God must believe that he exists and that he rewards those who seek him.

We must also love others and walk out our Christian life in love.

1 John 4:8

Anyone who does not love does not know God, because God is love.

The next step is belief. It does us no good if we simply have knowledge of God. Scripture tells us that there are many who know about God. However, to be a true believer, we must actually believe He exists in our heart and become obedient to His Word. It is only then that we can accept the free gift of eternal life given by God.

Romans 1:21

For although they knew God, they did not honor him as God or give thanks to him, but they became futile in their thinking, and their foolish hearts were darkened.

John 3:16

For God so loved the world, that he gave his only Son, that whoever believes in him should not perish but have eternal life.

It is this process that gives us the title of children of God, as we are born again into His new life.

John 3:5

Jesus answered, "Truly, truly, I say to you, unless one is born of water and the Spirit, he cannot enter the kingdom of God."

Finally, if we want to really find God, if we truly want to experience all of the promises that He has given in His Word, then we must seek Him with all of our heart, soul, and mind.

Deuteronomy 6:5

You shall love the Lord your God with all your heart and with all your soul and with all your might.

Jeremiah 29:13

You will seek me and find me, when you seek me with all your heart.

I can tell you that without my walk with God, I would not be here today. God has carried me, helped me, met my needs, healed my mind, provided for my family, and shown Himself to be true in many other ways. Like many of you, I am a walking testimony of God's faithfulness. In fact, it is hard for me to understand why people don't believe in God.

That is why it is so important for each of us to know why we are Christians. It is not based on our church attendance or how much we put in the offering. It is based on the things that I have shared in this book. Faith, trust, belief, hope, salvation, and so many other aspects of who God truly is. Without Him and His divine intervention on our behalf, each of us would face an eternity full of darkness and suffering. Fortunately, we have a loving God who made a way for us to enter into His life and walk in His light, a way that is available to all mankind if they will just accept and believe His truth.

WITHOUT HIM AND HIS DIVINE INTERVENTION ON OUR BEHALF, EACH OF US WOULD FACE AN ETERNITY FULL OF DARKNESS AND SUFFERING.

BATTLE PLAN

WE MUST

1. Share our faith and our testimony with unbelievers. Make a practice of looking at others with God's perspective every day. What does He see in them? What is His plan for their life? How can we be used by God to influence them and lead them closer to Him?

2. Share our faith and our testimony with other Christians. Each day we come in contact with believers who may be struggling. We can you pray for them. We can share a testimony of what God has done in our lives or how He is using us in current situations. Testify of His greatness and His salvation.

3. Learn to be bold enough to walk out our Christian belief each day. We are not to hide our light under the bushel basket, but we are called to be the light of the world.

4. Walk out our faith and our belief by fulfilling the call of God to all believers. That is to share the Gospel with all mankind.

Don't be afraid, warrior. It is time to enter the battle and let God take control of the outcome. Remember, He promised to be with us always—even to the end of the earth.

The non-existent enemy, this is a dangerous and useful tool of evil. It is the ultimate lie that can carry a person straight to the pits of hell. This is why it is so important for us to study God's Word and know why we believe in the things of God.

In our world today, it is imperative that the true believer be able to stand and give account to the purpose and source of his or her salvation. Unfortunately in my travels, I have found that many people who claim to follow God are unable to give a solid reason for their belief.

Remember: Going to church doesn't make you a Christian any more than going into a garage makes you a car.

What is my definition of a Christian?

_____

_____

_____

_____

_____

What is the biblical definition of a Christian?

_____

_____

_____

_____

_____

What has happened in my life that makes me able to call myself a Christian? (1 John 2:6, Ephesians 5:1–2)

_____

_____

_____

_____

_____

What work or effort did I put forth to obtain my salvation? (Ephesians 2:8–9)

_____

_____

_____

_____

How does an unbeliever accept Jesus as Lord? (Romans 10:9, Acts 2:38)

_____

_____

_____

_____

How do I find common ground with a stranger and develop an instant relationship so that I can talk to them about God?

_____

_____

_____

_____

Explain how prayer can be used as an evangelistic tool of opportunity with someone I meet?

_____

_____

_____

_____

_____

_____

FINAL THOUGHTS

If you are a true Christian, you are absolutely required to share the gospel with the world around you. They may not all get saved, but that is not your responsibility. Your responsibility is to tell them about Jesus. The rest is up to God and the free will of each individual. (Mark 16:15, Matthew 24:14, Psalm 96:3, Matthew 28:19–20)

In this area of ministry, do not start coming up with excuses. I have heard them all. "I am not good enough," "I am not a pastor," "I don't know enough Scripture," "I am scared to talk to people," "I don't know what to say," "I just witness by the way I walk out my faith," etc.

You can say whatever you want, it will not change the words God will have for you when you stand before Him. Each of us is accountable for what we say and do, and what we do not say and do, according to God's Word. This is not my opinion; this is God's command (Matthew 28:19–20). Therefore, for a Christian it is a non-negotiable attribute of their position in the family of God.

Friend our world is going to hell without Christ. People around you and me are dying every day and spending their eternity separated from God. It is time for us to stand up and be counted.

All of those excuses mentioned make this whole thing about you. Well, here is a news flash—nothing in this is about you or me; it is about Jesus. So let's just get out there and do what we are commanded to do. Let's be bold enough to walk down the path that was designed for each of us by God. By doing so, each of us becomes one of the few who are willing to stand up for God, and we will fulfill His promise of using the remnant to accomplish amazing things.

Throughout Scripture (both Old and New Testament) and history, God has used people like you and me as prophets, disciples, evangelists, and a host of other messengers for His kingdom. He chose us to do so because of our tenacity and unwavering commitment to His kingdom. No, we may not always say or do it 100% correctly. However, if we are obedient to His divine call, He will use us to reach those who may not listen to any other voice.

Remember, you are uniquely qualified to reach into the lives that God has destined for you to touch. He designed you in that specific way for a very specific purpose, and you can reach people with your personality that would turn away from my kind of approach. Therefore, please take what you can from this book and this teaching, as God uses you to do more than you could ever ask or imagine according to His will and His divine plan. (Psalm 139:13-14, 1 Peter 2:9)

PLEASE GOD, AND YOU WILL BE REWARDED.

My prayer is that while reading this book you have found special ways to connect to God and His divine plan for your life. I realize that some of the things I shared may be offensive to others in different ways. However, in writing these pages, I have never had the intent to hurt anyone. I have only attempted to use a direct and honest approach to bring understanding to the spiritual battle we face. At times, those attempts may have seemed abrasive. However, if we look at Scripture, we see that even Jesus was abrasive at times. Not everyone liked Him, and if you read the whole story, you will see that even the religious Jews called for His crucifixion.

There is one fact about the way I believe that I often share with others. That is that there is only one person you or I have to please because there is only one person that will allow us to enter into the gates of heaven—and His name is Jesus. It will not be our churches, denominations, pastors, friends, or family members that will open that door. In addition, it is not our job, donations to ministry, titles, or anything else we do on this earth that gets us to heaven. In fact, Scripture says that it is by no other means than the work of Jesus Christ on the cross. Therefore, be at peace with all men as much as you can, but in the end, please God, and you will be rewarded.

Another thing to be careful of is comparing your work for the Lord with the work of another Christian. As a warrior of God, you have a different assignment than I do. In your effort to complete that assignment, do not worry if it appears to be greater or lesser as compared to the assignments given to other believers. It is like the task of a military or paramilitary unit—each person has their job. Some are snipers, and others breach the door or wall for entry. One person on the team provides direction to the team from the front on initial entry (#1 in the line), while another covers the rear of the unit (watches our six so no one can sneak up behind us). You have team commanders, team leaders, and team members. Regardless of the position and title, each one has their specific duties and responsibilities. Without each one doing their specific assignment, the team is at risk.

So, wherever you line up in the overall scheme of things, just remember to do your part and stay in your lane. You are gifted in many ways, and your gifts are different than the gifts of someone else. However, your gifts have been given to you because that is who God made you to be in this life. Therefore, be who He has called you to be and do not try to conform to what everyone else wants. That will end as a lesson in futility.

Remember, God loves you just the way you are, and He will use you to complete His will for your life. He has a plan for you, and He will bring it all together in His perfect time.

May God continue to richly bless you in all that you do according to His divine will. Be bold and be strong because God is with you, and He will never let you go.

ABOUT THE AUTHOR

Jerry Peters, Jr. retired in 1999 as a result of injuries sustained in the line of duty as a United States Marshal. He is founder and director of Operation Life Support and Integrity Ministries. Both organizations focus on helping other through the trials of life and crisis events, in addition to encouraging a stronger walk with Christ. Jerry is also an ordained minister and a chaplain. He has held positions as a senior pastor, missionary, evangelist and keynote speaker. His mission is sharing the Gospel of Christ with the lost and encouraging believers to greater obedience to God. His goal is to use his many life experiences to help others understand the mission that God has for their life as they develop the warrior spirit that all believers should exhibit.

During his career as a United States Marshal, Jerry was involved in many high threat assignments that included: witness protection, fugitive apprehension, dignitary protection, anti-terrorism, and other mission related duties of his position. During that time, he developed a sense of honor and duty to the United States that still exists today.

However, his career also exposed him to an overwhelming view of the despair and hopelessness that exists in every part of our world. After experiencing personal tragedy, God placed a desire in his heart to help others. This has been accomplished by combining his Christian upbringing, spiritual sensitivity, tactical training, and street experience. God has given Jerry a direct and honest approach that is effective in ministering to people and encouraging them to a closer walk with Christ. This approach allows him to share God's message of hope to the hurting and the lost. Just as God has promised, God has taken a tragedy of life and turned it into an opportunity of ministry for the glory of His kingdom.

In recent years, Jerry has continued his commitment to our freedoms by working under the U.S. Department of State in support of anti-terrorism programs. These programs help other nations develop the personnel needed to fight this plague of destruction that affects our entire world. As a subject matter expert, Jerry has assisted in the development of programs related to anti-terrorism, counter-narcotics, tactical response (SWAT), border security, and dignitary protection. In addition, he completed three tours in Afghanistan as an embed advisor, providing services through Department of Defense and State Department programs. These positions have allowed him to not only raise the necessary funds to operate the non-profit organization mentioned, but also afford him great opportunity to minister and share the message of Jesus Christ with military personnel and others throughout the world.

Jerry views this ministry effort as a mission. It is a mission to win the lost and revive the church. A mission that will result in eternal goals as directed by the will of God no matter what the cost. He has taken his attitude of the warrior spirit and redirected it from serving Country to serving God. He uses the same aggression toward his spiritual enemy that he used against those who were the enemies of the people of the United States of America and the world.

Throughout his life, Jerry and his family have endured many tragedies, including the combat disability of their son during the war in Iraq. In all of the tragedy that Jerry has faced, he has learned this one important message: God has a plan that has been promised to each of us in Jeremiah 29:11-14, "'For I know the plans that I have for you,' declares the Lord, 'plans for welfare and not for calamity to give you a future and a hope. Then you will call upon Me and come and pray to Me, and I will listen to you. You will seek Me and find Me when you search for Me with all your heart. I will be found by you,' declares the Lord, 'and I will restore your fortunes and will gather you from all the nations and from all the places where I have driven you,' declares the Lord, 'and I will bring you back to the place from where I sent you into exile.'"

CONTACT INFORMATION

If you would like more information about this career warrior, please send an email message to *TacticalChristianity@Outlook.com*. This communication line is open to share your salvation experience, tell how this book motivated you, schedule guest appearances or speaking engagements or plan retreats. These opportunities allow him to share his personal story, motivate your group, and share the needs of our soldiers and first responders. You may also order books or devotional materials as they come available and follow his ministry at *TacticalChristianity.com*.

"MAY WE NEVER FORGET THOSE WHO SACRIFICE FOR OUR FREEDOM."